I WATCH
YOU SLEEP

*A Doctor's Tales of Anesthesia
and Chain Restaurants*

Zach Antonov, MD

Disclaimers

To maintain the anonymity of the individuals involved,
I have changed some details.

These are my memories, from my perspective, and
I have tried to represent events as faithfully as possible.

Some scenarios in this book are fictitious. Any similarity
to actual persons, living or dead, is coincidental.

Paperback KDP ISBN: 9798806425608

For comments or inquiries, contact the publisher at
ZachAntonovMD@gmail.com

Cover art by Daniel Weiner. Find him on Instagram @repeatart

For all the patients of the world, and the physicians who take care of them.

TABLE OF CONTENTS

INTRODUCTION

Santa Claus and I have a lot in common. We both watch you when you're sleeping, and we know when you're awake. We both provide nice girls and boys with goodies—Santa with candy canes, and me with lidocaine.

And we both have giant sacks.

Thank you, I'll be here all night.

Medicine has forever had a mystique about it. You go to the doctor, retain maybe 20 percent of what is said and done there, and spend weeks fighting your insurance company about some charge. If both you and the doctor perform your roles well, you're able to magically slow the inexorable decline of the pile of flesh and bones you call your body. Sometimes doctors do more than prevent; sometimes they cure. They can figure out that some cells in your body are going on a rampage and multiplying uncontrollably, and then make it all go away. That's some crazy shit when you think about it. Physicians and nurses are in your favorite TV shows, dramatically yelling mysterious terms and acronyms and saving lives.

They're on the news, too, sometimes being depicted as healthcare heroes, but oftentimes as symbols of greed, arrogance, and corruption. Everyone thinks they heard from a friend of Nicki Minaj's cousin that they know some doctor with a giant house, a Ferrari, and a vacation home in Bermuda, who is in Big Pharma's pocket and gets paid money every time they kill someone with a vaccine.

My specialty of anesthesiology is particularly mysterious. Everyone can comprehend on some level what it means to have a surgery performed on them— cut skin, take out the bad, fix the good, close everything back up. And for the most part, that's pretty accurate. Sorry, surgeons, it's true! But for most people, when it comes to anesthesia, the span of time between when their eyes just start fluttering closed on the operating room table and when they wake up in the recovery room is just a black box, a Schrödinger's cat situation where they are both alive and dead. What happens while you're asleep? Does the anesthesiologist pat himself on the back for finishing his job and leave the room to drink coffee and check on his stock portfolio? Does he just sit in the room on cruise control, writing the next great American novel? Does the staff start a bonfire and perform the customary presurgical ritual of sacrificing a virgin (I've managed to evade my own sacrifice so far) and begging the gods for another uneventful appendectomy? Only two of those things have some basis in reality, and I'll let you figure out which ones they are.

Let me take you on a little journey to give you a sense of this crazy life in anesthesiology and medicine. You will get a sense of my own personal trajectory and of the stupid things I find funny. All the medical stuff in this book is true, based on my own experiences and those of close friends and colleagues in the field. I will do my best not to shy away from any issues or controversies in medicine, such as finances and the rise of nonphysician practitioners. Sometimes I exaggerate things to make certain points, but never at the expense of data or accuracy; I even include footnotes when relevant![1] Everything else, however, is questionable, sarcastic, and dramatized. I'm a failed standup comedian who fell into medicine as a backup, so this is my creative outlet. I use the F-, S-, B-, D-, and P- words freely and in various eloquent combinations.[2] If you get offended or shocked, then I have succeeded in my storytelling. Bear with me as I inevitably get sidetracked and discuss other subjects important to me, like food, sex, and movies, though not necessarily all three at the same time. I hope what you get out of reading this is a deeper understanding and appreciation of the medical profession—anesthesiology in particular—and

---

1 Like this one! But with actually useful information or data...
2 Fuck, shit, bitch, dick, and pussy, respectively.

perhaps more importantly, I hope you get some laughs and have a good time.

And I hope you tell all your friends to buy this book, of course.

1. THE ORIGIN STORY

Y ou need to understand the process of becoming a physician. The path walked—or rather, crawled through in agony—by every doctor. The origin story. If the doctor you see in front of you is the movie *The Mummy* with Brendan Fraser, then in order to get a good grasp of how they became the person they are, you need to see *The Scorpion King*. The doctor's backstory could indeed be just as painful as that film.

The true origin of the desire to heal people comes much earlier than school age. It must, because no one would choose this field with its associated sacrifices and struggles willingly and rationally, looking over a list of pros and cons and saying, "Yeah, I think I'll be a doctor instead of an electrician." The profession of "doctor" has magic even as a child. When you ask a kid what they want to be when they grow up, "doctor" is an answer in such esteemed company as "firefighter," "pilot," and "dinosaur." Before even knowing what a doctor does, outside of some vague idea of saving people, some children instinctively gravitate to it.

When I was young, I grew up with little children's encyclopedias and cutesy books about the human body, along with the prerequisite plastic toys and tchotchkes. No one in my family was a doctor, so I certainly wasn't coerced down the medical path. I think they simply thought those things were cute; how amusing to see a little child reading about bones and blood vessels instead of little blue trucks. Having been born outside of the United States (I emigrated when I was about three years old, having decided it was time for a change), you would think I'd have the usual immigrant parent pressures on my ultimate career choice. The stereotype of immigrant parents disowning their children unless they become either a lawyer, a doctor, an engineer, or in the case of Jonny Kim, a US Army lieutenant, physician, and astronaut, does indeed ring true for some, including some of my own friends.[3] I get it, the whole "we work our asses off so you can be successful, and the only measure of success is these three occupations" thing that parents do, but I didn't get hammered by that as a kid. I just seemed to naturally gravitate towards things relating to the human body; I found it fascinating.

---

3 Jonny Kim is indeed a real person. He started out as a soldier, then graduated Harvard Medical School, and then decided he just hadn't done enough with his life and became an astronaut. The gold standard by which all immigrant parents judge their children now.

By the time I got to college, I more or less knew I'd pursue becoming a physician. College is really the latest you have to decide this, since you need to take numerous required classes, such as physics, chemistry, and biology, as part of a pre-med track. Some people don't feel a calling to medicine until later in life, at which point they have to go back and take said college classes, and then they're valiantly chasing their dreams while being that weird old guy in a class of twenty-something-year-olds. Other countries require that commitment to medicine a lot earlier; European medical schools are basically six-year combination college/med school programs that start after high school.

I can almost guarantee that no high school or college student who pursues a career as a physician truly grasps the consequence of that choice and what the road entails. How can someone comprehend the extreme stress, eight plus years of extra education and lost income, and massive debt, when their current priorities in life are getting laid and figuring out which sandwiches are currently buy one, get one free at Subway? I think the medical profession relies on this blissful ignorance and that childhood sense of awe to recruit more people, because if those applicants knew how broken the current US medical system can be at times, they would strongly reconsider their career choice.

You get a taste of the high-stakes nature of medical education during college, when you prepare to take the Medical College Admissions Test, or MCAT for short. (There are a lot of acronyms in medicine, so get used to it now.) It's an eight-hour, $300 exam consisting of questions about chemistry, physics, biology, sociology, and critical reasoning. Every US medical school requires it as a criterion for admission, and if you screw up and get a low score, good luck finding any medical school that will accept you; forget about top-tier ones. This is just the beginning of the reconstruction and remodeling of your life, transforming you from a complex, multi-faceted person into someone whose only identity is medicine, whose worth is only measured by a test score.

Can you imagine how disheartening it becomes when, throughout your entire educational and professional life, you are solely judged by a metric? MCAT scores, shelf exam scores, med school class grades, multiple board certification exam scores—I could go on. In fact, I will! Patient satisfaction scores, hospital discharge times, operating room block time utilization. Although a person cannot be distilled to a set of numbers, that is precisely what medical schools and insurance companies do because they do not have another way to judge a doctor. You can be the most motivated person, driven by an altruistic desire to save people courtesy of some sob story about your grandma dying and you wanting to make sure no other grandmas die ever again, but if you have subpar scores, those are all an admissions committee will see. It is unfortunate because I know many people who are great clinicians and educators but who are unfortunately poor test-takers, who have had to struggle constantly with the Sisyphean task of proving themselves to everyone throughout their careers. Conversely, there are plenty of fucking idiots that get into med school—they've been great at taking multiple-choice tests their whole lives—who I can't imagine ever being given the responsibility of caring for another human being. They probably think they're hot shit, too, because they've cruised through their education riding on their high scores. It's an unfair way to judge someone's capacity to be a competent physician, but as of now, there are sadly no other easy, fast, standardized markers of "intelligence" that interested parties can use to quickly filter through candidates.

College ended up being a lonely time because of all the studying and pressure. Do I go out and make friends and party, or study and volunteer at a hospital? It didn't help matters that I lived off-campus, taking the subway every day from Queens, where I lived with my mother. I had plenty of time to myself to study at home (in between my mother's horrific alcoholic benders), and the few opportunities I had to make friends were often squandered because it took so much effort to take a bus and two trains into Manhattan, especially late at night. Much easier to learn the Henderson-Hasselbalch equation at home while petting my cat.

I once took a survey at my college where one of the questions was, "Think of your six closest friends. How many of them attend this college?"

There was no answer choice for, "I don't have that many friends."

2. P. F. CHANG'S, OR PTSD

After my first taste of the score-boners everyone would have throughout the rest of my career, I started medical school in Syracuse, a modestly sized city in upstate New York. Since I grew up in New York City, I felt like I was in the middle of nowhere. I had to drive everywhere, and the closest *anything* was always fifteen to twenty minutes away, regardless of where you were, like some boring suburban *Twilight Zone* episode. Most lamentably, the pinnacle of cuisine in the area was [insert your choice of generic American casual dining chain restaurant here]. For instance, allow me to digress and regale you with the tale of my transcendent first experience at P. F. Chang's:

Asia has a very rich, long, and storied past. I knew this because in junior high school they said so, then moved on to teach us about all the better achievements of America. Though I had been dating an Asian woman for about two and a half years at the time, eating all of her family's unfamiliar, delicious foods, I still felt very much ignorant of Asian cuisine and culture, so what better place to eat a mid-week lunch than P. F. Chang's China Bistro?

Accompanying me on the journey was my Chinese friend, whom I asked to guide me in my culinary expedition through this foreign cuisine. Upon being seated, I realized she was the only Asian person in the entire restaurant; there wasn't even a stereotypically-dressed Asian hostess in the front to make passersby become intrigued by her exotic Oriental beauty and by the smells of MSG wafting from the kitchens.

Upon opening the menu, I was hit with a sense of nostalgia. It was like Mr. Pontius Frederick Chang knew of my longing for New York City Chinese take-out places and made his entire menu a glorified representation of them. Fancy-named versions of my favorite, completely non-diarrhea-inducing take-out dishes like Beef and Broccoli, Shrimp and Broccoli, Broccoli and Broccoli, and Salt in MSG sauce practically jumped out of the page at me, begging to be ordered. I also noticed some clever wordplay in some of the menu items, referencing the stereotyped barebones history that the clientele may not even know; the most prominent one was the Great Wall of Chocolate, but I'm surprised such vegetarian classics as The Yellow Turnip Rebellion and Pearl Onion Harbor, or the sandwich classic Hero-shima, weren't on the menu.

Our waiter came over with a plate of three sauces for the table and began explaining to us what each of them was.

"This dark sauce here is a potsticker sauce," he began with a most delicate and loving voice. "It's good for many of the things on our menu." I had heard of this strange invention known as "soy sauce" before, but I'm glad he cleared things up for me.

"This next sauce is a thick red chili sauce," he continued, "and it's very spicy, so be careful!" Good thing he didn't confuse me with the pronunciation of its name: sriracha.

"And this here is a green horseradish sauce, sometimes known as wasabi. Now, what I like to do is mix it all together to make a 'special sauce.'" He looked both of us in the eyes as he slowly stirred the spoon in the bowl and lightly moaned, demonstrating how to properly mix.

The entrees arrived surprisingly without a tolling gong to signal their coming. The Dali Chicken, though not initially spicy, had a spice that, according to my friend, "kicks in later"—on the toilet, I assumed. My own Orange Peel Shrimp felt at home in their natural environment, because they were swimming in a sea of thick, super-salty sauce; any edema I may have had was sucked right back up into my veins. The Asian-Grilled Norwegian Salmon looked like standard fare you would get at any steakhouse since it was lacking any sort of Asian flare. I'm assuming it was cooked on a grill made in China, though, so the name fits. It was underdone in the middle, for which I'm glad, because I got the best of both worlds—seared salmon and sashimi! Come on, Pontius Filibuster Chang, get your shit together!

With the check came our fortune cookies, signaling the restaurant's authenticity, but I'm surprised statin drugs didn't accompany them. My fortune was, "You have a heart of gold," and I smiled because they misspelled "salt." In the end, my guide told me that she thought it was fancy takeout food. I urged her to be quiet lest she ruin the illusions of the diners around us; it was our little secret.

I bet you're wondering how this memory is so vivid. Certainly the food wasn't amazingly delicious nor horrifically disgusting enough to leave an imprint on my memory. But the four-year span of medical school is a time unlike any other. It is grueling, which I'll describe soon, but also magical in the way it transforms you as a person and etches certain memories from that time onto your mind. Of course I learned about the significance of the ECG, which I still carry with me to this day, but the experiences I had, both inside the hospital and out, are the things that stick with me the most.[4] Maybe it was a coping

---

4 You can sometimes see the word *electrocardiogram* abbreviated as EKG, for *elektrokardiographie*, the German word. Don't say it around your great-grandpa who fought in WWII.

mechanism for the PTSD suffered, a natural instinct by the bruised and battered brain to trick me into thinking med school was enjoyable, filled with fun, food, and friends. Regardless, my mind happened to frame my time in med school (and beyond) around shitty chain restaurants, so reading about them is critical to show you my state of mind back then.

Oh, who am I kidding? Not much has changed since.

Usually, the first two years of med school are classroom based, consisting of classes teaching microbiology, pharmacology, physiology, pathology, anatomy, analysis of medical literature, patient interaction, and more. The days started early for my classmates and me, shuffling to campus from our houses or apartments in the frigid dark before the sun had a chance to creep over the horizon and laugh at me for choosing this insane life. Throughout the day, we would bounce between different lecture halls, classrooms, standardized patient exam rooms, and labs to attend our classes.

The sheer volume of information thrown at us throughout medical school, especially those first two years, was staggering. Have you ever drank from a firehose? Me neither; that would be stupid and irresponsible. But learning all that material felt like I was Joey Chestnut stuffing my mouth with hot dogs of information, hoping to sweet Jesus I'd keep at least some of them down. Many of the things we learned were important and relevant, while others seemed pointless and unnecessary. I understand the importance of knowing how kidneys filter the blood and what can go wrong, but why did we have to memorize the Krebs cycle and which substrates were needed to make acetyl-coenzyme A[5] for the ultra-rare inborn errors of metabolism that most doctors will never see in their lives, unless they decide to specialize in the field?

I do understand that the choice of what to teach in medical schools is a delicate balance between producing doctors competent in the realities of clinical medicine and crafting physicians who are knowledgeable about everything under the surface as well. Physicians are meant to be true mental powerhouses, the final stop in the medical journey. Even though we may not remember what the cause of acute intermittent porphyria is, physicians are expected to at least know *of* it, know that it exists, maybe even remember the vague symptoms, and be able to know what to do or who to consult next. This expansive knowledge is also needed for more common ailments, like hypertension. Anyone can learn how to prescribe a few medicines for high blood pressure, but *why* does the patient have the disease? Is it the typical stiffening of the blood vessels with age,

---

5 The Krebs cycle describes how our cells make their fuel and energy. There are eight steps with a ton of complicated enzymes and substrates. I had to Google this all over again, which shows you just how unimportant these kinds of things are to the majority of clinical medicine.

poor diet, and lack of exercise? Or could it be the rarer case of pheochromocytoma, an adrenal tumor that cranks out epinephrine to jack up the blood pressure? If this patient were given a standard blood pressure cocktail and told to exercise more, instead of being worked up further, given the appropriate medicines, and scheduled for surgery, he or she may die. This burden placed on physicians is large, but it is what drives us to keep learning and to be the best doctors we can be.

3. THE CHEESECAKE FACTORY, OR ANATOMICAL GIFTS

A *brief history lesson: The Cheesecake Factory was a relatively recent addition to my med school town and the first Cheesecake Factory in the whole region. Anticipation was high during the construction of it (in the mall, where else?). Locals seemed more excited about the opening of the Cheesecake Factory than the opening of the new Cancer Center at our hospital. On the fateful day, the first customer camped out for the grand opening for five hours. I'd tell you about the two health inspections the restaurant had failed to pass, but no one cared.*

My girlfriend came to visit me on Independence Eve, and I thought, what better way to show her the embodiment of my town than to take her to the

Cheesecake Factory? I decided to invite two of my friends as well.

After buying some Crocs while waiting to be seated (gotta love mall restaurants), we finally headed inside. The place was huge—grand, dare I say. To go along with the large surroundings, we were each given copies of War and Peace. I didn't remember the novel having so many pictures, and only later did I realize that these manuscripts were the menus. Never before in a restaurant menu had I actually seen advertisements. Surprisingly, none of the ads were for statins or insulin.

It took us about ten minutes just to figure out our drink orders. Being a little bitch, I opted for a nonalcoholic fruit drink, and most of my table actually followed suit; one of my friends wanted to one-up us on the diabetes and got a Dr. Pepper instead. We got mango, peach, and "tropical" flavored iced drinks, though if they were mixed up, we wouldn't even have tasted the difference. Two of the drinks had some kind of red swirl inside, which may have been drops of blood from the drink maker's fingerstick blood sugar test.

During our hour-long deliberation of what we should order, many internal struggles were fought. Seafood or landfood? Pasta or sandwiches? Butter or more butter? One of the burgers was called an Old Fashioned—I was glad this place served their burgers with a side of manual stimulation. Also, a pasta dish *called Evelyn's Favorite Pasta; who the hell was Evelyn, and why did I need to care?*

Eventually, we decided. We got an appetizer called Factory Nachos first. Why was everything in this place associated with a factory? Wasn't this the opposite of what most people wanted? This implied that the nachos and cheesecakes were just being mass-produced by little Cambodian children who, just like the cream cheese they concocted, got whipped nonstop. But when you really thought about it, was an artisanal product, handcrafted by someone excited to get up in the morning to go to work, that much better? I didn't think so.

The Factory Nachos were factory loaded with all the good stuff you would expect—cheese, chicken, guacamole, sour cream, salsa, jalapeeenyos. They were a good start to a meal and probably would have been a good end to a meal as well under normal circumstances. But being in upstate NY was not a normal circumstance, so we pushed onward.

Our entrees came out, and we gots to samplin'. The Shrimp and Chicken Gumbo was buttery, spicy, and flavorful. The Shrimp and Chicken Jambalaya, which was basically like the previous dish but in a different shape, was luckily good as well, with the chicken being exquisitely tender. I got the Bistro Shrimp Pasta, which consisted of heavily battered and fried shrimp on a bed of angel hair pasta with a lemon garlic cream sauce. My friend's steak and mashed potatoes dinner was pleasant; the potatoes were very chunky and more "smashed" than "mashed" if I had to say, and the steak was well cooked. Each of these entrees could easily have fed an entire child factory worth of workers, and only one of us could finish a portion. I had to take a mid-dinner bathroom break to unload my excess baggage and make room for dessert. The bathrooms had Dyson Airblade dryers, which automatically made a restaurant great in my book.

And of course, we had to get the eponymous cheesecake. There were two pages of these bad boys on the menu, making decisions very difficult, but we settled on an Old Fashioned (no hand job included), a Dulce de Leche, and a Kahlua Coffee Cake. Each of them was a varying level of good, but the Old Fashioned strawberry was my favorite. The cakes were creamy and lived up to my high NYC cheesecake expectations.

This was my first Cheesecake Factory experience, and I left content. My girlfriend left even more content because she basically ate my friend's cheesecake and took her own piece home. Good prices, big Central New York–style portions, and most importantly, good friends.

If you had to name the most quintessential medical school class, the one that fully encapsulates the entire med school experience, the one that diffuses into media and pop culture, you'd probably say anatomy.

If you didn't, then fuck you; pretend you did so we can move on. There's a macabre fascination that nonmedical folk have with the thought of students slicing open a dead body, dissecting away muscle fibers, crunching through bones with clippers, and sawing off the skull, and with good reason. It's not exactly something an aspiring TikTok star would make a video about, though probably more for legal rather than moral reasons.

The practice of dissection for medical education started with physicians robbing graves for their cadavers, then progressed (if you can call it that) to morgues and prisons selling their unclaimed dead bodies to the highest bidder, and eventually came to resemble its present state, where many people make it known in their wishes and wills that they want their bodies donated to medical institutions for education. It's a very noble thing to give one final gift to aid in the formation of young doctors, especially if you know what goes on in the lab.

Anatomy is taken seriously by everyone involved. On the first day, the smell of the lab hits you hard and burns your nose—the acrid odor of the preservative used to prevent rot. The lab is pristine, gleaming, sterile, and filled with neatly arranged rows of metal tables with a shrouded body on each. The instructors make sure you know what a gift and opportunity it is, made possible by someone's selfless generosity. For a lot of students, this is their first time seeing a dead body. Some get emotional; some get nauseated or faint. The faces of the cadavers stay covered with a cloth or sheet during most of the dissections to try to make everyone forget that there was a person in that body once.

Although personal details about the cadavers, like names, are not given—maybe only an age and a cause of death—the act of dissection becomes a very intimate experience. Sometimes we discovered things during dissection that hinted at the person's health: a black, Swiss cheese pair of lungs presumably from a lifetime of smoking; a golf ball–sized tumor in the intestines that may or may not have killed the person; a sclerotic, pinhole-sized aortic valve that was a ticking time bomb.

Occasionally we would see personal details on the bodies. One of my cadavers had fiery red nail polish. Why was she dolling herself up? Was she preparing to go out somewhere and have fun, when death came unexpectedly? Some bodies had tattoos, tracing a small, beautiful map of the meaningful moments in their lives. One of the bodies had a penile implant, a device that lets one get an erection at the push of a button. What kind of shenanigans did he get up to with his bionic penis? Was it one of his party tricks? And I know what you're wondering: no, the implant doesn't still work when you're dead. Little details like these really helped ground us throughout the year, to always remember to treat the bodies with respect.

Once all of the seriousness and shock value of working with dead bodies is out of the way, however, everyone gets comfortable and settles into a routine over the course of the class. There's a saying, first uttered either by me or Plato, that people can get used to anything, and dissecting cadavers is no exception. It is just the start of the process of acclimatizing doctors to blood, piss, shit, vomit, snot, mucus, pus, and organs. Eventually, anatomy becomes just another class. Another chore. Another test to spend hours stressing over and studying for. You find ways to keep sane and entertain yourself. Crude jokes fly freely.

The majority of mnemonics used by us are dirty. For example, to remember whether each cranial nerve carries sensory data, motor data, or both, the popular mnemonic is, "Some say marry money, but my brother says big boobs matter most," where the first letter of each word tells you the function of that numbered nerve. To remember the names of those pesky cranial nerves, we use the mnemonic, "Oh, oh, oh! To touch and feel virgin girls' vaginas and hymens" (olfactory, optic, oculomotor, trochlear, trigeminal, abducens, facial, vestibulocochlear, glossopharyngeal, vagus, accessory, hypoglossal). Having trouble remembering all those bones in the wrist? Well, as you know, "Some lovers try positions that they can't handle" (scaphoid, lunate, triquetrum, pisiform, trapezium, trapezoid, capitate, hamate). We are all just children, developmentally stunted by our long education.

You may find the vulgarity hard to believe, or think it's disrespectful. "It's not becoming of doctors!" But it's a natural way for humans to adapt to new and stressful situations. You wouldn't want a surgeon frightened and scared when they're operating on you. We do what we must to get by.

At the end of each year, the anatomy class would hold a memorial service, the Anatomical Gift Ceremony. This was an event meant to commemorate the people who donated their bodies for our education. There were speeches by the anatomy department along with poems and music performed by my co-students, and a presentation of a large mural created by us. Everyone was serious and respectful, because a number of the donors' families were in attendance. I can't imagine how these families must have felt, listening to their father/mother/brother/whoever being praised for their devotion to medical education while knowing it entailed a bunch of twenty-somethings staring at their naked bodies and dissecting them apart over the course of the year. The donors' remains were cremated at the end of each year's class, to provide the families some physical memory of their loved ones, and these were presented at the ceremony. It was very moving, providing a reminder to us that what we do is almost a sacred privilege, as well as giving a sense of closure to the families. But would I donate my own body for this cause after my death? I don't know; I don't have a penis pump, and there's not much else to look at down there. If I knew people were laughing at me, I'd just die.

...Again.

4. THE OLIVE GARDEN, OR I AM NOW WITHDRAWING

I *knew what my life was missing: class. Refinement, elegance, a certain zhe nah say kwah. With food dubbed "casual," I figured finding such class might have been difficult, but lo and behold, standing proudly betwixt a Taco Bell and a check-cashing place: The Garden of Olives. To assist my friends and me in such an endeavor—a type of dining I was hitherto unaccustomed—I recruited a person well-versed in authentic Italian dining, my friend Pierce. His credentials were extensive enough to easily put him a hair above the one other person in consideration; not only was he an overprivileged Italian-American wanksta from Long Island, but he also spent two minutes browsing Wikipedia finding out what authentic Italian food was like.*

It was a good thing an expert was in our midst. He came appropriately dressed in an oversized Carhartt tee, making me feel embarrassed in my fashionable winter garb. Right upon entering the Garden of Olives, I gasped and felt transported to an Italian villa B-movie film set. Adding to the old-world ambience was a wine-tasting table near the hostess. Good thing, since keeping up with tradition, I had to wait half an hour amidst the throngs of Syracusans waiting to be seated to get their unlimited breadsticks. I beckoned our resident expert on some things Italian over to the wine table to try its offerings. He was immediately carded. Great start. Pierce sampled the newest white wine in the Garden's collection, a nice, full-bodied 2014 Porto Vito Bianco and very much enjoyed it, remarking that it was good, in a Welch's 100% White Grape Juice kind of way.

After finally being seated, I opened the menu to gaze upon the offerings. I was immediately thankful for the smart menu design, because not only did it contain the names of food categories in Italian, but it had English translations right next to them as well. English was my first and only language, and I refused to learn anything about any other, because if everyone else just learned English, we'd all be fine. Thanks to the menu, I learned that pizze translated to pizza and could proceed, finally knowing what all the gibberish meant and knowing that I was a goddamn American.

Our waiter came over and introduced himself. His name was Chad, brah, and I wondered what exotic

Italian name "Chad" was short for. Chadolo? When it came time to order, I was torn. Should I order the Italian sampler, which included authentic Italian chicken fingers? I didn't know if it would come with some Sweet Baby Ray's BBQ sauce, so I refrained, and instead settled on calamari, fried zucchini, and stuffed mushrooms. The appetizers were thrown together haphazardly, making me feel cultured with their unique, abstract Jackson Pollock vibe. Luckily, they tasted better than they looked. To get a good insightful opinion from the Italian expert, I asked Pierce what he thought.

"S'good."

Thanks, buddy.

For my entrée, I ordered the shrimp mezzaluna (WHAT THE HELL DOES THAT M—oh, the menu said it means "half-moon")—ravioli stuffed with shrimp and cheese. Before they arrived, however, I had a critical decision to make.

"Unlimited salad, or unlimited soup?" Chadantini asked me. Well, hell, if I was paying money, I was gon' git some bang for my buck and eat all the unhealthy, creamy soup I desired. I could pick grass off the ground outside and make my own salad if I wanted. The various soups I tried were doused with heaps of freshly grated parmesan cheese and were, as expected with all things cheese-laden, satisfying. I was glad I had unlimited Victorian-era

dildo-looking breadsticks to dip into the hot, sticky cream.

The entrees finally came, and my friends and I dug in. I sampled their orders—the grilled chicken primavera lasagna was tasty for a "healthy" option, and the shrimp vesuvio was hot and spicy, just the way your mother likes it. My shrimp mezzawatchamacallit was rich and creamy, as I myself would be in old age. Many of the soups and entrees had pancetta in it, and I could tell they spared no expense getting the finest quality Oscar Meyer imitation of it because it was oh so salty and pleasing.

We contemplated ordering some wine to ring in the weekend, but all the great $20 bottles of Robert Mondavi, available on the bottom shelf of the liquor store across the street (right next to the aforementioned check-cashing place), were a bit out of our price range. On that note, when Chaddio brought our bill, I was a little shocked at the price. Twenty-two dollars per person? This was America, not Dubai. We reluctantly forked over the money, while Pierce continued to try to convince us to get wine, as he was a raging alcoholic.

I felt bad ignoring Pierce most of the night. He must have felt like the third wheel in a two-guy, one-girl threesome, awkwardly masturbating in the corner while his partners had at it. So to close out the evening and to get any other insight on the whole experience, I asked him to share his opinions with us.

"Was alright. I gotta take a dump."

Wiser words had never been spoken, friends.

The remainder of those first two years of med school did not have the shock factor of being elbows deep inside someone. (I'm talking about anatomy lab, you perverts.) The only shocking thing was the ridiculous amount of work and studying that had to be done. At the end of each semester, everyone's social media feeds would fill up with pictures of tall stacks of notes and material that were often multiple feet high. Med school exams and board certification tests were constant, a steady stream punctuated by the occasional grocery trip, restaurant outing, or trip back to NYC to see my girlfriend. We learned what felt like thousands of disorders—most named after esteemed doctors who were later disgraced for their beliefs or by being former members of the Nazi Party (of which there were surprisingly many).[6] Then, we had to relearn those damn disorders with their new names. Subjects blended together into a menacing hydra with as many heads as nephrons in the kidney. (There are about a million in each.)

---

6 Just some of the examples: J. Marion Sims is considered the pioneer of American gynecology, with common surgical instruments named after him, but he practiced his surgical techniques on black slaves without anesthesia; Friedrich Wegener, a former member of the Sturmabteilung (a wing of the Nazi party), had a disease named after him, which is now renamed "granulomatosis without polyangiitis"; Hans Conrad Julius Reiter's eponymous syndrome was renamed to "reactive arthritis" because of his Nazi associations.

Our education started to become more relevant in the classes about the practice of medicine—how to perform a physical exam on each body system, how to take a history, how to talk to patients. Because being nothing more than well-educated man-children (and woman-children?) we certainly needed a refresher on how to interact with people; something told me that although rapping Nicki Minaj's "Anaconda" with a patient I was evaluating in the emergency department probably boosted her spirits, singing about a pussy being called Nyquil due to its sleep-inducing qualities probably wasn't the most professional way to connect.

We worked on *standardized patients*, basically actors who played a certain part and let us perform physical exams. The most awkward part of those classes was learning the male and female "sensitive" exams of the breasts and genitals. We were actually provided lists of what to say and do and what *not* to say and do during them. For example, when removing a speculum, don't say, "I'm pulling out," but instead, "I am now withdrawing." One of the list items for the female exams actually advised against using colloquial terms for breasts. Like I was planning on entering a patient room:

"Hello, ma'am, my name is Zach Antonov. I'm a first-year medical student working with the doctor today. Would you mind if I palpated your sweet, juicy titties?"

The same list for males was pathetically short. Because women are precious, dainty things, and you must take special precautions with them, while no one cares about men. The no-no list for males may as well have said:

"Don't... rip his balls off?"

"Uhh... don't suck his dick?"

5. TEXAS DE BRAZIL, OR UROLOGISTS PLAY WITH *OTHER* PEOPLE'S DICKS

T*he life of a medical student was so depressingly long and arduous that it was necessary to break things down into the most minuscule milestones just to get an illusion of happiness and accomplishment. The preceding night's pointless milestone: finishing our last school exam before clinical rotations. Of course I hadn't forgotten about the much more important national exams that we had to cram for in five weeks, but my friends and I wanted to enjoy the moment. I figured a fancy celebration was in order, and lo and behold, it was once again in the mall: Texas de Brazil.*

For those of you not as linguistically gifted as I am, Texas de Brazil translates roughly to "Texas of Brazil." What does it mean? Does it mean it's a Brazilian restaurant filled with crazy, rights-denying

Republicans? Is it trying to imply that it is a combination of two places that have the biggest associations with copious quantities of meat? Or maybe it just tries to sound exotic with the "de" in the name while still being accessible to the local yokels.

Upon being seated in the restaurant, which was very sleek and trendy with dark woods and soft lighting, the servers... did nothing. We weren't asked if this was our first time at a churrascaria, and we didn't even get asked for drink orders. A churrascaria is a Brazilian steakhouse where servers with skewers of meat come around to the tables and slice you off pieces of the freshly grilled animals right on your plate, all you can eat. They know which tables to go to because of the medallion each diner has in front of them. The rules: flip your medallion to GREEN for "BLOCKADE MY COLON WITH JUICY MEAT," and flip it to RED for "OH GOD, NO MORE." This particular chain did not have rustic, wooden medallions, but little flimsy plastic things that looked like they were run through a girl's My First Laminator machine.

There was also a hot/cold food bar in the restaurant that offered things like salads, sushi, cheeses, oils and sauces, and a plate full of bacon, of course, because Syracuse. It even had lox, because as everyone knows, Brazil is home to the biggest Jewish population outside of Hollywood. Nothing was particularly great at this bar. In fact, the sushi, which had CHIVES in it for God's sake, was disappointing, and the lobster bisque, which looked more like Velveeta liquid gold, was unappetizing. Also, it seemed that about half of the items had capers in them, and I'm not talking about the Ocean's Eleven movies.

The servers additionally provided our table with fried sweet plantains and an obscenely delicious bowl of bread bites. I never thought a place would beat out Red Lobster in Best Pre-Meal Bread Offering for their lovely biscuits, but JESUS, this restaurant's delicate cheese-filled bread balls were good. The sweet plantains were obscene for a different reason, however. The restaurant must not have received the memo that sweet plantains are already sweet and don't need to be drenched in brown sugar. If we liked any of the above, we could ask for more, but that's how they get you. They try to lure you in with their delicious banana and balls so you stuff yourself before the barbecue. We fought the urge.

Then came the real stars of the show: the meats. Servers came around routinely displaying various types of meat on skewers, telling us what it was, and asking if we would like some. Throughout the course of the night, I had bacon-wrapped filet mignon, bacon-wrapped chicken, garlic sirloin, flank steak, pork ribs, beef ribs, Brazilian sausage (the server never called me the next day), parmesan-crusted pork, leg of lamb, lamb chops, and pork tenderloin. I felt like I was getting deepthroated by the cast of Orwell's Animal Farm.

Most were delicious, and all of the meats were seasoned fairly simply to bring out the natural flavor of the meat—lots and lots and LOTS of salt, and other light spices. I must have drank a gallon of water when I came home later because of all the salt. But come on, a little high blood pressure never killed anyone... right?

During the meal, the service redeemed itself a bit. Every time I got up to either get more stuff from the salad bar or purge in the bathroom, my napkin would magically be refolded upon my return. And people say there are no more miracles in this world. Our glasses were kept (mostly) filled with ice water, and the server did a great job explaining the dessert options to us.

One of my companions led us to believe that the desserts were included in the $45/person charge, so we went all out, but alas, we actually had to pay for it all. At least the sweets were enormous. We tried the key lime pie (fair), the citrus crème brûlée (we basically jizzed our pants when we heard the crack of the crust), the triple chocolate mousse cake (a standout), the cheesecake (eh), and the carrot cake (decent).

"It's not the best dessert I've had," a friend said. "In fact, it's just OK." Just saying, the latter would

have implied the former, so I chided him for wasting my precious damn time.

In the end, it turned out to be a good time, even though we could barely walk to the car afterward. My friend's comment of, "Dammit, I forgot my butt plug," perfectly summed up the feeling of being stuffed to the brim with food. I'm pretty sure I went into ass labor in the restaurant; I definitely had contractions and was at least three centimeters dilated. But with my last school exam done and enough meat to feed 2 third world countries in my belly, I happily said adiós!

... What?

They don't speak Spanish in Brazil?

The third year of medical school was the transition from classroom-based learning to clinical rotations. Over the next two years, we had to bounce around between Internal Medicine, Surgery, Pediatrics, OB/GYN, and Psychiatry. It was a Medicine's Greatest Hits album, though since we often did not know what we were doing, it was closer to a Kidz Bop version of one.

Medicine and its subspecialties were interesting simply because of the sheer variety of diseases and people we saw. We had the opportunity to rotate through cardiology, infectious disease, hematology/oncology, gastroenterology, pulmonology —you name a body system, and there was an -ology for it. Family Medicine involves every type of patient —womb to tomb—all in the same day. We could have been helping with a newborn exam, followed by a Pap smear, followed by helping a demented patient's family member figure out their goals of care. We learned in that rotation that every old person is in a perpetual state of "I'm Going on a Cruise Soon." And we, of course, did healthy numbers of genital and rectal exams, which we were expertly trained to do.

During one of my days in a Family Medicine clinic, I walked into the patient's room with the physician, was appropriately introduced as the rotating med student, and stood there as usual like a fly on the wall, watching the friendly banter between doctor and patient developed only after years of visits. Lots of "how's the daughter" and "your Yankees sure took a beating" types of remarks. The patient came for his yearly physical, and the usual things were done. A good history taken, heart and lungs auscultated. The perfunctory genital exam to check for hernias. A lot of med students are afraid of performing a penis exam because they're afraid of giving the patient an erection and being embarrassed. I was afraid of performing a penis exam for the fear that I would get the erection.

"Oh, sorry! Thought I was past the college phase!"

When it was time for the prostate exam portion, the physician asked the patient to bend over the table and motioned for me to come closer. There's a common saying in medicine used to illustrate the importance of the rectal exam, that there are only two reasons not to perform one: if the patient does not have an asshole, or if you do not have a finger. Given that neither of those criteria was met, it seemed I would not escape performing one. The doctor gloved up with a satisfying snap, lubed up his index finger, and entered. All as expected, but then he motioned for me to perform the exam as well, while his finger was still in there. So with my own gloved and lubed finger, I entered the patient's rectum, using the doctor's finger as a guide. It was a tender, magical moment, really: a mentor and his protegee, inside this guy's asshole. All we needed was Spandau Ballet's "True" playing on the overhead speakers. The patient was a good sport, and all he said was, "Oh! Looks like I got another visitor!"

Surgery was its own special type of hell, and we only got a taste of the insane lifestyle surgeons lead. We arrived at the hospital before the sun rose, and left after it set. I started to think daylight was just an urban legend, especially in the already dreary winters of Syracuse. The early mornings consisted of patient rounds, when the whole surgical team checks up on the patients on their service, but as med students, we were expected to pre-round and show up even earlier to see the patients, so we could present them to the senior resident or attending as we rounded. Rounds were always harrowing; it felt like standing naked on a royal stage, a burning-hot spotlight pointed at me, performing for the king.

"Um, Mr. Smith is post-op day two from his small bowel resection for obstruction. He is starting to pass gas and feels hungry. His labs are normal, and his vitals are stable. I think we should... advance his diet?"

"Hmm," the king would say. "But did you check his drain output to look for evidence of anastomotic leak?"

"No..."

"OFF WITH HIS HEAD!"

There were some bright moments. The entire surgery team was rounding on a particular man who was recovering from some vascular procedure, and because of his numerous medical conditions, he had a very edematous, fluid-filled scrotum, which caused him much discomfort.

"How are we feeling today, sir?" the attending surgeon asked the patient.

"How am I feeling? My goddamned nuts are the size of a grapefruit!" I had to leave the room because I could not stop laughing.

After rounds, we were split off between either assisting in surgeries or running the floor and seeing surgical consults. It's hard to say which one was the better option, because they sucked in different ways. If we were the floor bitches, we just wrote notes and maybe assisted with disgusting wound dressing changes. If we were in the ORs, we were standing in one place for hours on end without a piss break, retracting some organs or blood vessels so the big boys could see what they were operating on. On the rare occasion we were given the divine honor of cutting the surgeon's suture, it was always too long or too short. Throughout all of this, we would be peppered with medical questions by the residents and surgeons, quizzed on both the common and the esoteric. This infamous process is called "pimping" and is in theory meant for the physician to gauge the level of knowledge of their underlings, but in reality is a way for these doctors to feel empowered, to impress upon students how amazingly smart they are and how difficult their specialty is, and in some cases, to simply demean.

I enjoyed Surgery to an extent. In fact, I had entered medical school thinking I might pursue orthopedic surgery. However, after a few months of seeing what actually goes into being a surgeon, I decided it was not for me. I could not see myself as being the man. While I enjoyed the ability to pick the soundtrack for the OR (want to blast Ace of Base? No one will question you) and the technical aspects of surgery, I just did not think I could get to a skill level good enough to be considered an expert, and I did not want to do anything I could not do extremely well.

"If you can imagine yourself doing anything other than surgery, you shouldn't be a surgeon," a surgical resident once told me, referencing the intense drive and desire needed to be able to withstand the stress and workload of a surgical lifestyle.

At the end of my third year, I had to start thinking about which specialty I would choose. Always a daunting decision for medical students, it was particularly difficult for me. I thought the choice was supposed to make itself clear, to declare itself to me the first minute I spent in the specialty. If I wanted to be an obstetrician, I expected angels to sing and trumpets to sound when I delivered my first baby. If psychiatry was meant to be, I expected an orgasmic euphoria to come over me when I asked a patient about their mother. In reality, the decision for most med students is a pragmatic, carefully-weighed one. Most people like certain aspects of multiple specialties, or perhaps even enjoy more than one specialty equally. I liked the procedural aspects of surgery, along with the instant gratification of fixing something; following up with a patient in six months to see if a medication change was effective did not appeal to me. However, I also enjoyed the cerebral nature of medicine, the rumination and decision-making involved when confronted with complex issues. Which specialty could I pick that had all these elements I appreciated?

Anesthesiology wasn't a required rotation, but rather an elective week we could take within our Surgery block if we were so inclined. Figures, the first introduction med students get to anesthesiology is a perfect summation of the field: mysterious and hidden from view. I chose to do it because I certainly didn't want to do an extra week of the ICU instead, and because I heard anesthesiology was an interesting field. In my brief time in the operating rooms on the other side of the surgical drape, I finally got to see what the anesthesiologists were doing during surgery. Since it was only a week, I only got the basic gist of things: the anesthesiologists evaluate the patient preoperatively, induce anesthesia ("put them to sleep"), sometimes do procedures like intubation (place a "breathing tube"), and then keep the patient alive despite the surgeon's best efforts to achieve the opposite outcome. Over the next few years in medical school and residency, I would come to know that the process is a lot more complicated than that.

There is a lot of downtime for anesthesiologists during surgical cases, so I had the chance to talk with them about their life and how they came to their specialty choice. Certain professional points were commonly repeated:

"I liked procedures and the OR but didn't want to do surgeries."

"I liked pharmacology and physiology."

"I enjoyed the lifestyle."

"I dreaded the idea of wearing anything but scrubs to work."

Of the handful of anesthesiologists I talked to, none regretted going into the field, which couldn't have been said about other physicians I had met who regretted their specialty choice. All of the anesthesiologists just seemed... content. And that's what I decided I wanted to aim for in my life.

When asked which field I was planning on going into, I started to say that I was between something in surgery, and anesthesiology. I told a urologist that I was considering his specialty.

"Vell, you know vat ze only difference eez between urologists and anesthesiologists?" he asked in his thick Russian accent. "Urologists play wiz other peoples' dicks!" He chortled, and I returned an expected chuckle and also mentally noted this joke for any future books I may write.

Anesthesiology is frequently seen as a waste of talent by other specialties, which can be off-putting to a prospective propofol pusher. But then, every doctor shits on every other specialty and thinks any field but their own is garbage. If I went into surgery, the medicine doctors would make caveman noises to imitate surgeons. If I went into medicine, the surgeons would hike up imaginary glasses and try (and fail) to talk about something cerebral and medical. I quickly learned not to let others' opinions of a field influence my own thoughts and decisions.

After completing my main rotations, I took the plunge and focused my efforts on pursuing a career in anesthesiology. It was a scary decision, especially after only spending a week experiencing the field, but it had to be made early, so I could tailor my fourth-year schedule appropriately. I thought it wasn't a terrible choice, and I could certainly think of a lot worse ones, like neurosurgery. Plus I liked basically wearing pajamas at work, so if nothing else, at least I could look forward to breezy loins.

6. TILTED KILT, OR OVERPRICED LETTERS

The fourth year of med school progressed at a furious pace, filled with elective rotations, exams, and the dreaded residency interviews. I was so busy, I only had the chance to eat at one fine dining establishment. My friend suggested going to a very stimulating place, like Hooters, but I assure you I shot them down. Please, I did not need to have a side of female objectification along with my quintuple cheese nachos. So I decided on Tilted Kilt instead. Which was basically a Scottish Hooters. See the difference?

I dragged two of my buddies with me, and we trekked through the brutal Syracuse winter, ravenous in many ways. We entered the restaurant and were immediately greeted by the hostess, and she did indeed have the most-est. We were unlucky, because her breasts were not small and humble, and we did, in fact, confuse them with mountains. As she led us across the floor to our table, I looked out at the room and was surprised that there was not one female patron. I would have thought there would at least be some, who suggested the idea to their men only to chastise them when actually there.

Upon being seated, our waitress greeted us by providing coasters for our drinks. Lucky for us, her name was written on them, because lord knows no one hears the waitress's name as they are busy staring at her large... résumé. We asked our waitress how one gets a job like this, and she told her story:

"I asked if they had a job, they said yes. Then they made me go in the back room and put on one of these skimpy outfits, and when they saw me, they said, 'You're hired.'" Good for you, girl. Gotta pay your way through dental hygiene school somehow.

My friend got very flustered when ordering and had to apologize to the waitress for his severe performance anxiety; he was quite smitten by her, that hopeless romantic. The nachos were nothing to write home about (unless you frequently write home to momma about mediocre food), and the accompanying guacamole was bland, lacking the deeper citrus and garlic flavors I expected. My compatriots' burgers had a nice taste, but once again, no deeper flavors beyond "grilled meat in a bun." Points for the burgers actually being cooked to our specifications though. The accompanying fries were the stars of the show, especially the Sidewinder Fries, a thicker-cut take on zesty curly fries.

As for my entree, I decided I had to be as uncomfortable as possible while placing my order, so I turned to one of the innuendo-laced items. I had to choose between such perennial favorites as The Big Rack (ribs), the Double D Burger, and the One-Shot Johnny Shepherd's Pie. Ultimately, I decided on Sadie's Stuffed Breasts, a chicken and vegetable dish. Aesthetically it was unimpressive, with two quite small breasts not living up to their name lying on top of a bed of steamed broccoli, all smothered in a mustard sauce. I wasn't sure how to approach the dish, so I tried motorboating it, but ended up getting mustard everywhere. The chicken was cooked well, but as had been the case with the other food, the flavor profile was not rich.

The night we came actually happened to be trivia night. We joined and made our team name be "My Kilt Can Only Get So Tilted," but the DJ kept misreading it, first saying, "My Kilt Doesn't Get So Tilted," then "The Not-So-Tilted Kilts," eventually devolving into "The Tilted... Not Sos." Jesus Christ, this guy just didn't give a shit about his job. I'm sure he was distracted by the wonderland of scenes around him: men blatantly staring at waitresses' breasts as they talked to them; waitresses ranging in size from petite to plus-plus size but all having one... or rather, two... things in common; someone's toddler-age daughter running around the restaurant, no doubt training for her future job.

We ultimately had a decent time, but I was sure we could have had that anywhere, because we were awesome and fun. The food, which I supposed was Scottish themed only because they had a Shepherd's Pie on the menu (where's the haggis?!), was fair, and the environment was not one we were the most comfortable in, believe it or not, and we lost to another team in trivia because the goddamn last category was NASCAR, and of course everyone in goddamn Syracuse got the answer except us. Would we have returned to dine again? Only if we had won the gift card from trivia. Otherwise, my friend had to accept the fact that he could only give our waitress one type of tip that night.

The cornerstone of the fourth year of medical school is residency interview season. While my classmates and I did have other electives and rotations to worry about, they were usually somewhat more enjoyable since they were tailored to our ultimate specialty choice. Additionally, we had quite a bit of free time as well to travel and sow our royal oats, but the bulk of our mental efforts went toward preparing for the interviews.

It all seems like a circus when I look back on it now. We'd played the multiple-choice exam games, we'd applied to residency programs with the hope of getting at least a few interviews, and then, we'd traveled all over the country at our own expense to spend a day or two being judged by others. While we of course were being evaluated by the program directors to see whether we'd be a good fit for their programs and bring minimal embarrassment to them, we, for the first time, were in a small position of power. If you were a stellar candidate (by which I mean you had astounding exam scores), you basically had your pick of residency. Though I certainly was not a perfect candidate, I was in the running for the top-tier programs in New York City, and I struggled to change my mindset from, "Oh God, I'll suck your dick. Just please accept me into this program," to, "Let's see how *you* can benefit *me*." After twenty-six years of living my life trying to earn acceptance and approval, the tables were starting to turn the other direction, and that was hard to grasp.

Our fate was decided through a process called The Match. Every year in March, thousands of medical students across the US simultaneously find out which residency program they matched into, where they would spend the next three to seven years of their lives. You plug in your ranked list of choices into the algorithm, and the residency programs similarly rank their interviewed candidates. Then out pops a piece of paper on Match Day, and in front of all your classmates, you unfold the paper and see the name of the program and city that will dominate your life for years. There are tears—happy ones from the med students that get their first choice, and sad ones from those that get their last. The biggest soul-crushing blow comes to those who did not match into any program; these students are informed the week prior to scramble into any open spot in any specialty, unless they decide to instead spend the next year doing research, volunteering at a hospital, or Eat-Pray-Loving their way across Europe until the next Match Day.

Match Day came and went—I matched into my first-choice program in New York City—and after four brutal years of medical school, my colleagues and I finally obtained our medical degrees. As graduation approached, I couldn't help but reflect on the whole experience, but when I tried discussing the matter with my friends, I discovered that we all had difficulty articulating the precise concoction of emotions we were feeling. Most simply summed up the feeling as "weird." On graduation eve, however, I found myself in bed with tears rolling in rivulets down my cheeks, wondering how it could be so hard to explain why.

This difficulty stems from so many different aspects of the medical journey. One part is the arduous nature of the beast: the sleepless nights of study, the sacrificed relationships, the anxiety surrounding the constant exams. After years of what felt like martyrdom, our graduation felt like an admission of the strain under which we were placed—

a validation of it. A big, "Well, I'm glad that's finally over."

The sighs and tears we released were both joyful and bitter. We constantly questioned and doubted ourselves. What did I actually do to deserve this? What did a grade of "honors" tell you about me, when I had friends who put their entire being and soul into their work and only scraped by with a "pass"? Was I simply a professional test taker, trained my whole life to be proficient in the science of multiple-choice exams? We felt that once we entered residency, we would be found out for the impostors we were, and that the suffixes after our names were nothing more than overpriced letters. The one thing that comforted me about this self-derision was realizing that it showed just how intensely we desired to live up to and surpass the standards of being a physician.

Another component of graduation emotions—perhaps the most important one—was the loss felt at parting ways with our colleagues. The previous four years had felt like an academic war, and my friends were right there in the trenches beside me. The bond we forged was unique; I did not become close friends with many of my classmates, but I did not dislike a single one, a remarkable occurrence given the randomness of putting a class of 175 diverse strangers together. And I lamented leaving them. We were all going our separate ways for residency, seeds of physicians carried on the wind to far-flung states, and this forced us to realize that friendships and relationships were not cumulative like we had hoped for, but segmental.

We had our college friends, then moved on when we graduated. Then we had our medical school friends and did the same. Rinse and repeat for residency and each subsequent job. It was so easy in this modern world for the extent of our continued relationships to consist of simply liking an occasional social media post or picture, and I hoped that this was a filter the friends who truly mattered would get past. The tears I shed were for this loss and tough life lesson. But I knew for a fact that if I needed to call on one of these beautiful friends and colleagues, they would not hesitate to answer.

When I look back on medical school, I can't recall many specific events or memories pertaining to my actual education. Restaurants and funny anecdotes, sure, but not schoolwork. Tests came and went, clerkships did the same. But I find myself comparing medical school to remembering any book I have read: I would be extremely hard-pressed to tell you much at all about the plot of it, but I can vividly tell you the emotions I felt while reading and whether I enjoyed it. I would say medical school was like being forced to read the Bible in college for my literature class: I wanted to shoot myself in the face while reading it, but I turned out to be a better, more knowledgeable person for it.

7. PAPA JOHN'S, OR, MUSICAL CHAIRS ON THE *TITANIC*

A s a young lad, I frequently ventured out with my father John Sigurd Antonov III into the forests a few miles away from our Norwegian home. I still cannot decide whether I loved those days or hated them.

The forests were filled with verdant evergreen pines year-round; pine cones littered the forest floor, making traversing our trails a chore. We would hike into the forest depths to look not for the truffles which peppered the pine bases like nuggets of gold, but for the fragrant, earthy Norwegian cinnamon bark whose taste—and trade—sustained us. The spice grew only in the coldest, darkest parts of the forest, where sunlight could not besmirch its natural essence. My nose and cheeks would become cold and chapped, and Papa would pull a balaclava he made from the shorn wool of one of our lambs over my head. When we would actually reach the clusters of cinnamon pines, Papa would sit me on his shoulders so I could harvest bark higher up the trunk. I loved that.

But I hated home. Home was me and him and our lambs and old Sven to help with the processing of cinnamon. Oftentimes when I needed Papa to be home at a certain time for help with schooling or cinnamon work, he would instead arrive late, bearing the miasma of mead, the red of lost love and life injecting the whites of his eyes. I would hide in Sven's disheveled cabin to escape Papa's heavy tears and heavy hand. Old Sven would give me some slices of tomatoes to calm me down, knowing I liked the sweet, tart taste of these fruits he would obtain every week from a questionable fellow from Roma. The next day Papa would always apologize for being late, for letting me down, and I would have no choice but to return to loving him again.

One particular day in the forests, while we were scouring for cinnamon, I became very tired, as I was recovering from sickness. I did not want to become a burden to Papa, so I kept it to myself, but he was always perceptive and noticed. He told me to sit down against a cinnamon pine, to relax and breathe in the pungent aroma of the spice. He would finish collecting bark from the surrounding trees and return to me.

My eyes snapped shut as soon as he walked away. I dreamt I was an adult in a new, foreign land, where snow covered not trees and cabins, but concrete buildings and cars. I dreamt of strange cinnamon confections and Old Sven's tomatoes. I dreamt of Papa.

When I awoke, he was gone. Tears were leaking from my eyes, but whether from the cold, the strong cinnamon, or fright, I cannot say. I stood up and stumbled—my legs had fallen asleep just as I had. There was no one in the forest but a young boy, whose teary blue eyes and straw-blond hair were the only things visible through his wool balaclava, yelling, "Papa? Papa?"

I am in America now and a decade wiser. I think I may have found Papa. He seems to own a pizza shop; why he would be cooking Italian food is beyond me, but so are a great many other things. I worked up the courage to call one night.

It was not as I expected. I was forced to order food. A cheese pizza with Roma tomatoes, just like the ones Old Sven let me eat, and a Cinnapie, a small, sweet pizza flavored with cinnamon and cream.

But my mistake was in thinking Papa had changed. When I needed him most, on the eve of a great hunger, two and a half hours passed, and still no comestibles.

No food, no Papa, no love. I, once again through tears, had to call out to Papa, severing my ties and canceling my order.

I am still the child crying out in the forest.

It's hard to fully describe how daunting and mind melting intern year was. The first year of residency; the first year working with an MD after my name; the first year of having true responsibility for patients' lives. The few months between graduation and intern year were filled with both excitement and fear. I imagine it's how Alex Honnold felt as he looked up at El Capitan before scaling it without any equipment. Except if he messed up, only he would die, while if I messed up, multiple patients could.

In anesthesiology residency, intern year is a mishmash of the specialties deemed to be the important foundations of a budding anesthesiologist. Surgery, internal medicine, emergency medicine, ICU, and a little amuse-bouche of actual anesthesiology to remind you what you're training for. The official designation of an intern is a PGY-1, which stands for *post-graduate year*. As you advance year by year in residency, the number goes up; the poor, lost souls of neurosurgery go all the way up to PGY-7, if they make it that far without killing themselves. Anesthesiologists are special and have the more specific designation of CA, short for *clinical anesthesia*, followed by their year. As interns, we were called CA-0s. An appropriate way to start residency, being classified as zeroes.

As nothing.

July 1. The infamous day every year when fresh, baby-faced interns start shitting their pants and taking care of your precious meemaw in the hospital. I started my year with three months on the hospital medicine service. There was no transition period, no gradual easing into clinical duties. I got a white coat, two pagers, and an unnervingly thick stack of hand-offs shoved in my face, followed by a pat on the back. I was encouraged to actually come to the hospital the evening prior to get a "relaxed" hand-off from the soon-to-be PGY-2 that was caring for the patients before me. The term "relaxed" was accurate, but only for the departing resident, who may as well have thrown his papers in the air, jumped and clicked his heels, and yelled, "So long, sucker!" I was most certainly not relaxed learning about the ten patients I had to take care of a mere twelve hours later, especially when all of them seemed to be at death's door.

"The patient in 641B coded again earlier today, but they got her back," the departing resident casually mentioned. "Family still doesn't want to make her DNR, but you can try to convince them again tomorrow."

"Oh, great, thanks," I said. "Now, how do I log onto the computer, again?"

I stayed until 11:00 p.m. every day that first week, hit by the cavalcade of duties and notes. My co-intern and I cried more than once, overwhelmed by everything. I lost ten pounds in two weeks because I didn't have time to eat. Our attending bought us Dunkin' Donuts out of sympathy. I stopped grooming myself; a patient later referred to me as Dr. Shaggy, though whether in reference to my mop top or my dulcet reggae singing, I did not know. I made a list of the things I most looked forward to doing on my first day off:

Eating more than once per day

Drinking water

Answering the forty important emails that had accumulated in the past week

Going to the bathroom whenever I wanted

Sleeping more than four hours

Breaking down in tears without anyone around me

I blew past the eighty-hour workweek limit immediately. Since the early 2000s, work-hour restrictions were put in place by the Accreditation Council of Graduate Medical Education as a result of the high-profile death of Libby Zion, an eighteen-year-old girl who was believed to have died as a result of overworked and exhausted interns and residents. There are arguments for and against these restrictions, with those in favor of them citing cases like Libby Zion and tired-driving accident and death statistics, and those against them believing they actually lead to worse patient care and poorly trained physicians. It's hard not to feel that the opponents of work-hour restrictions think that just because they had to endure one hundred-plus-hour workweeks that everyone else does, too, and that these damn kids have to get off their damn lawns. But physicians *should* be experts, especially those in extremely technical and complicated specialties like the surgical ones, and restricting their work would indeed decrease the number of times they perform a certain procedure as a trainee. It's a fucked duality, wanting our nation's doctors to be of sound mind and body while also demanding almost superhuman skill and performance. Anyway, everyone always lied about their work hours if they broke the limit, for fear of repercussions.

A fair portion of the daily grind was filled with menial tasks. Do you really think mere interns would be given true life-or-death responsibility? Knowingly, at least? Some of the things on my daily to-do lists were, "Add mashed potatoes *with butter* to diet," and, "Order whole milk instead of fat-free." This is what I had gone to medical school for, baby.

When an actual medical task did come up, I was like a deer in headlights.

"The patient is in pain," I would think. "I should order Tylenol. But, wait, does he have any liver problems? What if he does and we just don't know it yet? Do any of his other medicines have Tylenol in them? What if I overdose him, and then he'll need a liver transplant and die, and then *I'll* die of grief and shame?"

Meanwhile if it were me in pain, I'd pop three Tylenols and an Advil and chase it down with coffee without a second thought.

The building of knowledge and confidence was a big part of intern year. Once I overcame the fear of even the most benign things, opportunities presented themselves to demonstrate my skills. A patient of mine on the vascular surgery service had gone into a supraventricular tachycardia (SVT), a heart rhythm that can lead to injury and death. Her heart rate was in the 150s, she was starting to become hypotensive, and she was beginning to feel faint. I knew from my training that this was a textbook indication for giving adenosine, a medicine that basically rapidly stops the heart for a second (or couple) and restarts it at hopefully the correct rhythm. The vascular surgery fellow who was at bedside balked at the idea, worrying that her heart would not restart at all. I persisted, knowing there weren't many other things to do, and if we did nothing, she would get worse quickly and need to be cardioverted, or "shocked", with electricity. Eventually, the fellow relented, saying if anything happened, it was on me, effectively wiping his hands of any responsibility. I put on defibrillator pads just in case, pushed the medicine into the IV, and watched her heart rhythm cease for a second, before starting up at a much slower and more ideal rate. The patient instantly felt better, the fellow grunted a single "hmph," and I felt like a boss. Then my pager buzzed, informing me that my other patient was demanding the *cherry* Maalox, not the *lemon* Maalox I had ordered.

That first year of residency truly was absurd, like a Dadaist painting but with lots of bodily fluids and death. To paraphrase one particular infectious disease doctor from the hospital (who interestingly was a hand model before he became a physician), it was like playing musical chairs on the *Titanic*. We worked so hard and experienced the most insane things on the spectrum of life and death, but everyone was hurtling toward the same fate regardless, some just faster than others. Sickness was the great equalizer. An example: I had the distinct displeasure of caring for some snobby rich-kid, a hospital board member's son, after he needed to have surgery. He was recovering comfortably on Twelve East, the fancy, cash-only unit that wealthy folks sprang for when they wanted to enjoy more privacy, bigger rooms, nice park views, and fancier food. However, the surgeon wanted him to have a bowel movement before discharging him, but the kid just would not shit. The surgeon decided on nuclear warfare and made me order three successive suppositories for him. I imagined them being brought to the kid on a silver platter, with the nurse snapping on white leather gloves as she prepared to shove them in. It didn't matter how much money or status he had. He was still getting his ass entered. Three times.

Ridiculous stories like these stand out the most. The "is this really my life right now" moments. As another example, while on the surgical service, I was prepping a patient in the operating room, a process which involved shaving his nut sack with an electric clipper. As I was buzzing off all the pubic hair and wondering whether it was best to go *with* or *against* the grain, the patient, still awake, looked deep into my eyes, straight through to my soul, and asked me in his amazing German accent, "Am I ready for burlesque now?"

After he was asleep, I was further tasked with placing a condom catheter on him. For those not in the know, imagine a regular condom with a gigantic reservoir tip, except this reservoir is for urine and not semen. As you can imagine, it's very difficult to stuff a flaccid penis into a condom, so my co-residents helpfully suggested to fluff up my new friend first to make it easier.

A standout memory from that year involved one of my patients—let's call her Edith—who was not necessarily of sound mind. Edith had a few psychiatric disorders, and her competency to accept or deny her medical care was questionable, which made treating her gastrointestinal bleed difficult. I had to do my best to convince her to allow the nurses to administer a certain acid-suppressing medication to prevent further bleeding. After being called overnight to evaluate Edith for complaints of chest pain, I had an experience that made me wonder how I got to where I was at that point, with my mind barreling backward to my birth, and fast-forwarding to me standing in front of Edith and her rolled-up ball of paper. Allow me to transcribe word for word the exact note my hand, feeling as if forced by some higher power, typed in her chart:

> At 4:20 p.m., I was informed patient complained of chest pain. EKG ordered, was unchanged from prior. I examined the patient and told her that her chest pain may be acid pain from her ulcer. She adamantly told me that it wasn't, because her stool did not have blood. She said, "Here let me show you," and pulled out a rolled-up toilet paper ball from her pocket and opened it to display a ball of feces. She spread it around with her fingers, saying, "It doesn't even smell like shit. It smells like horse manure," and told me to smell it. I refused. Patient was unable to be convinced to take Protonix. Settled for Tums.

I later learned that she died shortly after, of course; you can believe whatever you want, but if you have a bleeding ulcer and refuse proper treatment, you deal with the consequences. My note is part of her permanent medical record. Anyone who cares to look can read it and be regaled by my tale of the shit ball; I like to imagine some lawyer in the future will review the case and be forced to call on me to be a fact witness and read my note in front of a jury. As you can see, a part of Edith lives on in me, just as I live on in her medical record. We are forever intertwined. This connection, a fleeting moment, a two-minute encounter and a one-minute note, is just one example of the countless fleeting moments that, combined together, transform an intern into a physician. Every physician becomes who they are because of a multitude of their own Ediths.

Death becomes a familiar presence during intern year, teaching young doctors the important lesson that no matter how good they are, they will always experience it. My first real experience with death was during an emergency medicine month. I stood in the trauma bay of the hospital, watching snowflakes fall outside through the windows as we waited—a "red trauma," gunshot wound to the head, per EMS radio. We always refer to the diagnosis, not the patient, at this stage, when there is no person to know and when the focus is just on how to keep the diagnosis alive. Seeing as I did not have much to offer as a mere intern, I stood around twiddling my gloved thumbs, waiting for the gunshot to arrive. Since there were no diet orders to change or social workers to talk to, my minimal intern skills would prove useless in this trauma setting, so I was able to take a step back and observe.

The gunshot came rolling through our trauma bay doors a few minutes later, paramedics ventilating him. The usual things happened: airway, IV, catheter, monitors. Maybe I should have been interested in learning how to resuscitate a patient, but I was more interested in the story the paramedics were telling: this man's gunshot wound was self-inflicted. Apparently, this seventy-something man's wife had recently died, and a cemetery groundskeeper found him near her grave with a gun in his hand and a hole in his head.

As the physicians were shearing away the man's coat, the down feathers inside burst forth and filled the air, billowing gently downward, beautiful and grisly. I wondered if this was exactly how the snow was falling onto this man's head as he stood at his wife's grave and decided that he had nothing else in this world to live for. I wondered if his last thought was how beautiful the snow was. I wondered if he put the gun in his mouth first before deciding it might be better to put it against his temple. I wondered if the snow sizzled as it landed on the muzzle of the just-discharged gun. I wondered if he thought about his three adult children he left behind.

I just could not make sense of it. It was a mix of beauty, romance, disappointment, sadness, anger. A note was found in his pocket—not a suicide note, but one stating that he suffered from "heart problems and prostate cancer." These were the least of his worries in his short life at our hospital. I felt relief when he finally did die, since that is all he wanted in the first place. Instead, he had to take a brief detour involving endotracheal tubes, bladder catheters, pressors, radiographic scans, and dozens of mouths whispering, "What a shame..."

I entered medicine at a time when, just as I started to forget about the last resident that intentionally overdosed, I saw a headline about a medical student who jumped from the window of a dorm, and I continued on my merry way through med school and residency because none of that was real to me. But this man was real. I shed some tears for him because he deserved them. He was not a gunshot wound, but a forlorn man who lost the love of his life and promptly decided to end his. I sent out a text to my co-interns telling them that I appreciated all of them and suddenly felt extremely grateful for everything—for the diet orders that were never placed correctly, for the sleep deprivation, for my colleagues, for the privilege to experience stories like these.

For life.

8. CICIS PIZZA, OR THE MICHAEL JACKSON

During a visit back to Syracuse, I decided to get the ol' food gang back together. It had finally come to this. The ultimate zenith of our excursions. Growing up in NYC, I had actually seen many commercials for Cicis Pizza, and they always looked so enticing. All-you-can-eat everything, cafeteria-style, for less than a copay of generic Lipitor? They had me.

In Syracuse, the world was my oyster. Cicis Pizza was finally within reach. I convinced my friends to go with me using the siren's song of unlimited pizza. We arrived on a Friday evening (but not too late, because this place closed at 9:00 p.m.) and pulled into the scenic parking lot. Cicis was in a secluded strip mall off a highway, flanked by such high-end establishments as Ollie's Bargain Outlet and Razer Lazer Tag. There were about six or seven other cars in the entire parking lot, so I steeled myself for a long wait to be seated.

We entered the restaurant, and it was filled with one large, lonely person eating in the far corner. Luckily though, we were able to be seated... but not before paying first. This concept was strange to me, but I quickly got through my discomfort when I realized it was only $5.99 for all-you-can-eat variations of dough, sauce, and cheese. The cashier swiped our credit cards and asked my Guyanese friend where he was from, because he "knew a guy from Africa with a similar name... from Bangladesh, in fact." I felt honored to be served by a savant with an encyclopedic knowledge of geography.

The place was set up like a school cafeteria, albeit with lower-quality food. So basically a prison lunch line. There were many varieties of pizza sweating oil under an electric sun all along the far end of the restaurant, with soup, salad, and pasta stations as well. We were very fortunate that there was only one type of soup, one type of pasta, and two types of sauce available, because if we had to add choice and variety to the heaping mountain of crap and responsibility on our shoulders already, we would have asphyxiated right then and there.

I unfortunately started with a cheeseburger slice, which was slightly better than a Pomeranian taking a little dump in my mouth, so I supposed that was good. It had ketchup on it; nothing more needed to be said,

77

especially to my fellow NYC brethren. The Hawaiian slice was actually decent, which was as big a compliment as this place can get. However, my friend went above and beyond and called the soup "mad decent." Give this place a Michelin star.

There was a pizza called a Hog Wild pizza, which we had to get. We had to have it fresh made since it wasn't available on the heating racks, and when it was ready, I was surprised that they didn't start striking a triangle dinner bell, yelling, "COME 'N' GIT IT." The pizza was topped with bacon, ham, sausage, pepperoni, and broken dreams. It was salty and fatty and in some sense delicious, but it was way too intense. I wondered how many customers sprinkled extra bacon bits from the salad bar onto their Hog Wild pizza.

The pasta bar was, as I mentioned, lacking variety. There was only fusilli pasta, with white and red sauces to complement it. They were extremely unoriginal and boring, just like how my life felt being in Cicis. I did, however, use the opportunity to dip my pizza into pasta sauces. That's when I knew I had made it in life.

There were actually some desserts too. The cinnamon buns exuded oil at the slightest poke and definitely did not have enough hot cum sauce on them. The apple pie pizza made up for that, though, as it had molten sugar and butter piled three inches high on a little crust. It was so sweet that it hurt my tongue.

By the end of the ordeal, all four of us had oil or sauce stains somewhere. We started to leave, full and mostly unsatisfied, but I thought I'd still give it a decent rating on Yelp, since it was so cheap. As we left, the cashier yelled, "Cici you later!"

So never mind. Pasta la vista, bitches.

Once I crawled past the finish line of intern year, the real action began. Anesthesia, baby. The thing I'd actually signed up for. When friends asked me what I did for a living, I became more confident calling myself an anesthesiologist instead of saying something like "intern" or "resident." Though the firehose of information pointed at my face during those remaining three years was even larger than the already formidable one during intern year, I was its sub, enjoying the pain, since it was information on something I cared more about. The final three years turned a boy into a slightly more mature and much more knowledgeable boy.

Much like in their fantasies, anesthesiologists have their fingers everywhere, in every part of the hospital. We care for patients undergoing surgery in the ORs, we perform labor epidurals and provide anesthesia for C-sections, we can provide critical care in the ICUs, and we must be able to respond to emergent intubations and codes anywhere, from a hospital room to the outpatient office across the street. Flexibility and adaptability is a strict job requirement; plans often change at the last minute.

The bread and butter for most anesthesiologists is providing anesthesia for surgeries, but although to us it is so normal and oftentimes boring (if all is going well), it is a scary unknown for most patients. Allow me to walk you, generic faceless and nameless patient, through the process of some routine surgery, like a hernia repair. By the time I see you in the pre-op area, you have likely already seen the surgeon at least a few times through office visits, developing a rapport with them and entrusting the physician with your bones, organs, or penis, depending on the surgery (and your gender). You more or less understand the procedure to be done, along with its risks and benefits. Now here I enter, wearing a tie-dye paisley scrub hat with some overgrown locks sticking out from the sides, surgical mask obscuring all but my baggy eyes; all you really have to go on to guess what I look like is my decade-old glamor shot on my ID card. At this point, you almost have no choice but to entrust your life to me if you want your surgery completed, and I have only a couple of minutes to earn that trust.

People joke that anesthesiologists choose this field because they don't have to talk to patients, since they're asleep, but getting to that point involves short and intense conversation. When I am asking you questions about your health, I'm like a homing missile zeroing in on the important things that are relevant to the anesthetic, such as major heart or breathing problems, while avoiding miscellaneous debris such as how bad your cat allergies are or that your second cousin twice removed was nauseated once after anesthesia. I have to figure out how best to disarm you (Humor? Seriousness? Spirituality?) so you can tell me what I need to know to keep you safe, while also instilling confidence, in a few short minutes. Maybe I'm just one of the few anesthesiologists that enjoys the talking part.

I ask you to confirm your name and date of birth (for the thousandth time), as well as the procedure being done and which side—one of the many checks to make sure we're doing the correct thing to the correct person. After introducing myself and my role, I ask about the obvious medical issues, such as heart and lung disease (Ever had a heart attack or stroke? Any asthma or sleep apnea?), and other less obvious ailments that impact my caring for you: any uncontrolled acid reflux that would increase your risk of choking on your vomit during induction? Does your rheumatoid arthritis involve your neck, which would make it harder to intubate you? I then perform a focused physical exam, listening to your heart and lungs as well as evaluating your airway. Open your mouth wide, stick out your tongue, show me how far back you can extend your neck. Do you have any loose or fucked-up teeth that could fall out during intubation and drop down your trachea like Wile E. Coyote, whistle and all? If I feel mischievous and want to see how long and mobile your jaw is, I ask you to bite your top lip with your bottom teeth.[7]

After obtaining all my desired information, I explain to you what will happen during the anesthesia part of the surgery, and its associated risks. Some less serious risks are post-operative nausea and vomiting, a sore throat from the breathing tube that you had, and damage to your lips, teeth, tongue, or throat from the process of placing the tube (we're very careful though). A not uncommon risk, unfortunately, is a scratched cornea, either from us not being careful in our treatment of your eyes after you're asleep (we are extremely vigilant about this and tape your eyes after you're asleep), you trying to rub your eyes like an idiot immediately after waking up in a delirious state, or some combination of both. I also explain to you that the more serious risks of anesthesia, such as problems with your heart, lungs, and brain, or even death, are extremely rare, but they do exist out there in the world. For example, if this is your first anesthetic, how would anyone know if you're one of the .001 percent of people who get a rare, life-threatening reaction called malignant hyperthermia? Or if you have a small hole in your heart that hasn't given you any reason to know about it, until an air bubble in our fluids crosses it, goes into your brain, and strokes you out? Or if you have a severe allergy to a drug we use? Modern anesthetic practice has become so safe that it's basically a given

---

7 You just tried to do that, didn't you?

that you will come out of anesthesia perfectly fine, but as the New York Lottery slogan goes: "Hey, you never know."

One risk you may ask me about is awareness under anesthesia. You may even tell me that you "woke up in the middle of surgery once," or know someone who did. Anesthesiologists take these claims very seriously because true recall and awareness— being completely aware but unable to move while feeling the excruciating pain of surgery—is extremely rare but potentially traumatizing to the patient. Since it's so rare, it's difficult to pinpoint an exact incidence, but some studies have estimated it to be about 0.001 percent of anesthetics. The risk is higher for situations such as trauma (since the patient is so unstable and dying that it's hard to give much medicine without killing them), emergency C-sections under general anesthesia (we have to induce anesthesia and take baby out within seconds to keep it alive, which can happen before mom becomes completely unaware), and cardiac surgery (putting a patient on cardiac bypass introduces so many variables that it's sometimes difficult to gauge anesthetic depth). The truth behind the vast majority of the "awake during anesthesia" stories is often a result of improper expectations, either assumed by the patient, set by the anesthesia provider, or a combination of both. Many times, the patient was aware or awake during a procedure which was performed only under moderate sedation, such as a heart catheterization or the busting of a kidney stone, in which case the goal was not to "knock someone out," but merely get the patient comfortable enough to do a low-pain procedure. In that situation, it is reasonable and even expected for the patient to be somewhat awake enough to respond to stimulation and even follow some commands. Occasionally, a patient says they "woke up" during a colonoscopy, conjuring images of the patient suddenly opening their eyes, pulling the scope out of their asshole, and jumping off the table. Once again, the reality is tamer and more understandable. Endoscopy is commonly performed under very deep sedation, almost at the level of general anesthesia, albeit without an advanced airway in place; the patient is usually breathing on their own. However, since it's not true general anesthesia, where a breathing tube would be in place and we would have more methods available to judge anesthetic depth, the propofol doses are ultimately a judgment call: give enough until you fall asleep and attempt to keep you there. Sometimes patients wiggle around a little or start deliriously reaching for the scope, in which case we quickly administer more sedation. However, colonoscopies and endoscopies can also be done under moderate sedation, or even awake without any drugs at all; a patient once requested no anesthesia for his colonoscopy because he needed to be able to drive his wife home that day after her own colonoscopy. If that isn't true love, I don't know what is, though I feel they should have just skipped the theatrics and bought a double-ended dildo. Anyway, this shows that even if a patient did come to for a tiny bit, no harm is suffered.

Once the operating room is ready, we take you there and give you some relaxing medicine along the way, usually Versed (an IV version of Xanax or Valium). If at the end of the whole shebang you don't remember much after that point, you can thank the Versed for providing the anterograde amnesia, and you can thank me for giving it to you, since I do love praise. In the OR, we move you over to the operating table, put on some cold monitors (get ready to hear everyone tell you it's like having a NASCAR pit crew working on you), and have you breathe in some oxygen through a mask. No funny business or anesthesia gas, only 100 percent oxygen, just like the good stuff you would pay for in oxygen bars in Vegas, except ours is plastic rather than blueberry flavored. Once all the oxygen is in your lungs and the nitrogen is out, I give you the sleepy medicine.

We have numerous medication options depending on things like the type and length of surgery, as well as the degree of terribleness that your health is in, but the most common drug we use for induction of anesthesia is propofol. That white stuff that sometimes burns as it goes in your veins. Milk of Amnesia. The Michael Jackson.[8] We use it like water, and the

8 Michael Jackson's death was ultimately ruled a homicide due to the inappropriately high levels of propofol and other drugs being administered by his personal physician as sleep aids.

craziest part is that we still don't fully know the exact mechanism of how it works, even though it's been in use for decades. Don't worry, though, a lot of medicine is like that. It's magical how powerfully and quickly propofol acts, and I still get a giddy rush when I push it and you fall asleep. I have experienced it twice in my life so far for procedures, and it feels as though you close your eyes and open them one second later to find that hours have passed and you're in the recovery room. Poor-man's time travel. Just like all of our medicines, we have a general range of weight-based doses that we use to determine how much to give you, but it's still a judgment call; younger patients, kids, and for some reason redheads, tend to need higher doses to knock them out. Finally, redheads have something to brag about other than Ed Sheeran. Older, frail people or those with serious medical issues need less. Anesthesiologists often joke that just showing a decrepit, on-death's-door patient the syringe of propofol is enough to induce anesthesia.

After you're asleep, and after I tape your eyes closed to protect them from scratches, I often have to assist, or entirely take over, your breathing. The airway is one of the most important factors anesthesiologists consider about a patient. Some would say that anesthesiologists are the masters of the airway; perhaps ear/nose/throat surgeons may disagree, and I invite them to kindly shut the fuck up (but help me with an emergency tracheostomy when needed, of course). For many procedures, we need to paralyze your muscles after you're asleep to help the surgeons do their thing, necessitating the placement of some kind of apparatus to take over the function of your useless diaphragm. Even if we do not paralyze you, being under deep anesthesia often depresses your drive to breathe and leads to weak, shallow breaths if we do not provide extra assistance.

Sometimes we place an endotracheal tube, a long hollow plastic tube that can be placed through your mouth or nose, or even directly through your neck in an emergency, that sits below your vocal cords. We like this. It is our gold standard. Ol' Faithful. It reliably protects your lungs from any mucus or crap that comes up from your stomach, and it is fairly secure. But it does of course have some risks, such as a sore throat and damage to wherever it goes, like your lips, teeth, tongue, and vocal cords. Sometimes we use something a touch less invasive and less secure—a laryngeal mask airway, or LMA. You can think of it as a plastic balloon with an air channel in it that sits behind your tongue, providing some assistance without the potential trauma of a tube, but sacrificing the security and protection of one. Sometimes we don't place anything at all and let you breathe by yourself, but we are always prepared to secure your airway in a pinch. In rare scenarios, placing a tube before you go off to sleep is the safest option, such as if you have a terrible-looking airway or you just broke your neck and keeping it as still as possible is of utmost importance. We numb up your airway and give you light touches of sedation as needed to make the whole process relatively smooth in experienced hands.

With your airway taken care of, I do a few more miscellaneous things, depending on the nature of the surgery. I often put a special plastic blanket on you that circulates hot air inside it to keep you warm. I give you antibiotics, if indicated, to reduce the risk of infection with surgical incision. I can put a gastric tube through your mouth or nose to suction out the air and stomach contents. In certain circumstances, I can place an arterial line (a special type of IV that goes in an artery and watches your blood pressure in real time, instead of waiting every so often for a blood pressure cuff to cycle) or a central line (a large form of an IV that goes in a large, central vein, such as the jugular or femoral, to provide fast and reliable access for medicines and fluids). I administer medicines to attempt to reduce nausea for you afterward. Overall, my goal is to purposely bring you to the brink of death, since that is what anesthesia is in a way, and keep you there, making sure you don't cross that threshold despite your body's and your surgeon's best attempts to kill you. Sometimes this involves giving you medicines to treat derangements in blood pressure, heart rate, pain, sedation, paralysis, blood sugar, potassium, calcium, magnesium, and many others. Often I fiddle with the ventilator settings to achieve optimal oxygenation and ventilation for you specifically. The art-rather-than-science side of medicine pops up as I make preparations to emerge you from anesthesia and extubate you; my goal, after safety, is to make it as smooth a ride as possible. In an ideal scenario, as soon as the drapes come off, I call your name, you open your eyes, and I take the breathing tube out. Reality is often rockier than that, but we still get that tube out at the end... most times.

If you are so sick, your respiratory status so terrible, that I deem I cannot safely remove that breathing tube, I can elect to leave it in and keep you sedated. I would transfer you to the ICU, where you would be monitored, and once you regained hemodynamic and respiratory stability, the ICU doctors would remove the tube. Often we have a good sense of the likelihood of this possibility before starting the case and are able to counsel you and your family accordingly.

In the majority of normal situations, though, I take the breathing device out at the end of the procedure, take you to the recovery room, dust the dirt off my shoulder, and congratulate myself on another job well done. I am in charge of your recovery room stay ultimately, which comes into play if you have persistent nausea or poorly controlled pain, or if something a little more serious happens like you trying to die. I try to see you before you leave the recovery room to go either to your hospital room or home, but even if I do, you likely won't remember much of that conversation afterward anyway. To you, our brief, drug-filled time spent together, combined with my milky white skin, makes me, in essence, a ghost.

As I said before, anesthesia has become so safe thanks to numerous technological and medical advances (many from anesthesiologists themselves), that no one expects anything less than mundanity. Everyone expects patients to survive, to come out the other side the same way they came in. The only time anyone truly remembers the anesthesiology team is when bad outcomes occur. It's extremely rare for any patient to be appreciative of the fact that we anesthetized them for a monster of a surgery and got them out alive, balancing their myriad severe medical issues, transfusing blood, and doing procedures, if they got a corneal abrasion and have a scratchy eye for a few days. Or if they got a cut on their lip. Or if their tooth got chipped. We anesthesiologists are like hockey goalies—we can't win the game; we can only lose it. Everyone expects perfection, and this is not unique to anesthesiology, for every physician bears this burden.

A neighbor recently asked me if I liked my lawn mowing service and if I would recommend it, and I thought, "I don't fucking know. I don't notice any problems, and that's maybe the best compliment you could give a service like that." And I realized anesthesiologists are similar in that sense; everything is simply "fine" until a problem is noticed. It is unfortunate that anesthesiologists, and I'm sure many other physicians, are judged instance by instance; it's not unusual to hear patients saying how horrible their anesthesiologist was because, for example, their epidural didn't work. In other professions it may be more reasonable to pass judgment like this; if a contractor works on your house and the whole thing collapses, or the lawn guy treats your lawn and it all dies, you can pretty confidently say that they are not good at what they do. But medicine is so intricate, with so few absolutes and so many variables, that the worth of a physician has to be measured over time. Did that epidural not work because the doctor was unskilled, with a history of poor epidural placement and function? Was it the more likely scenario of the patient being six hundred pounds with severe scoliosis, in which case no one in the world would have gotten it in without X-ray vision? Or was it simply poor luck, with everything looking like a good indicator of a functioning epidural but failing anyway for whatever reason?

The field of anesthesiology is often compared to the aviation industry, due to the high-stakes nature of their practices and the ultimate priority of safety. While I am only responsible for at most a handful of patients simultaneously, and pilots for hundreds, it is still a delicate, sometimes stressful situation. The induction and emergence of anesthesia can be likened to the takeoff and landing of an airplane, in that these are the times we have the most say over how the whole experience will go, and the times with the most potential for issues. Everything in between is "cruise control," though that is, of course, understating it, as I hope you see by now. But both anesthesiology and aviation have nailed down the processes and safety checks so well that, once again, everyone expects nothing less than perfection. I'm sure pilots often navigate their magical flying machines thirty thousand feet in the sky through intense storms and use their well-practiced skills to get everyone safely to their destination, but goddammit, your seatback entertainment screen was discolored, so you better write a letter of complaint instead of a letter of admiration.

Let me tell you a little secret: I want perfection too. I want to do all I can to make sure all of my patients wake up in just the same state as when they went to sleep, with no nausea, pain, scratched eyes, cracked lips, missing teeth, sore throats, or blown veins. But this is impossible. The human body is not a piece of machinery that humans themselves built. Each one is different, and there are no instruction manuals. The patient is not a machine that can be mastered, and I am not a machine that can consistently deliver perfection each time.

It is often said that the practice of anesthesiology is 99 percent boredom and 1 percent sheer terror, a slight exaggeration meant to highlight that while safe and boring the vast majority of the time, anesthesia can present great difficulties. For example, if you've ever wondered how quickly one can shit their pants, I invite you to perform anesthesia on a healthy child whose heart rate suddenly drops to zero.

Some of the greatest challenges are those faced during the care of very sick patients: the ones who actually worry me and whose anesthetic plan gets juggled around in my mind or tossed out to my colleagues for opinions, the ones who may not even make it out of the OR alive. I often lighten the mood with healthy patients who are anxious about the anesthesia by saying, "If I'm not worried, you shouldn't be worried. Now if the anesthesiologist were worried, then you should be." No one wants to be in that second scenario.

Of course there are technical and intellectual challenges with sick patients, but the emotional toll is often even greater. When I am performing my preop evaluation on one of these patients, they occasionally ask me, "Am I going to die?" This bomb they hurl at me penetrates my armor each time. I know all the complications, and I have told them to the patient as well, letting them know how high-risk they are, that they may, in fact, die. But still they ask me, as if I am some fortune teller. The best I can do is offer a platitude like, "We'll take care of you the best way possible." I know they don't really expect me to know the outcome, and oftentimes they have a good sense of it themselves. When they ask that question, I think it's their version of reaching a hand out of the water and hoping someone takes it, and if they don't get pulled up, at least they will have drowned while experiencing a human connection. Sometimes I am, unfortunately, the last person they will ever see, staring down at them, my image warped and refracted through the plastic mask between their eyes. I try to instill confidence with my posture and mannerisms for them.

Sometimes my words are the last they will ever hear, and I try to make them count, telling them what they want to hear:

"Everything will be OK."

I don't always get to talk to the patient beforehand —they could already be incapacitated. I have to let my mind fill in the blanks and wonder. I wonder what was the last delicious food eaten by the nine-year-old boy who died on the OR table after being hit by a car in the street. I wonder when was the last time my elderly patient saw her family before she went to sleep for a hip fracture repair and never woke up due to a massive brain bleed.

It is occasionally my job to address someone's do-not-resuscitate (DNR) and/or do-not-intubate (DNI) status before a procedure. Not uncommonly, a patient has an existing DNR/DNI that is at odds with the nature of the surgery, and I have to sort all this out. Normally, a DNR/DNI means that if your heart were to stop or you were to stop breathing, you wouldn't want any invasive or heroic actions performed, such as chest compressions or intubation. The procedural setting is unique, however, in that the odds of successful resuscitation are a lot higher. If your heart were to stop at home, on the street, or even in a regular hospital room, it would take time for people to figure out that this happened, to get help, to figure out why this happened, and to institute appropriate resuscitation attempts. All of this takes time, and the more time someone spends without oxygen flowing to their brain, the worse the outcomes are. Now imagine your heart were to stop or something catastrophic were to happen in the operating room. We are monitoring you constantly, we have the resources and capability to start proper treatment, and in many cases, we are able to successfully reverse whatever insult occurred. If you had a severe allergic reaction to a drug we gave, we can give medicine to turn that around; if you vomited in the middle of a colonoscopy, we can place a breathing tube temporarily to protect your airway before removing it as you're waking up; if your heart is about to stop due to massive bleeding, we can give you blood products.

In order to perform a procedure, some degree of resuscitation must be allowed by the patient. Yes, I see your DNR/DNI, but we can't do your exploratory laparotomy without general anesthesia and a breathing tube; you're welcome to bite down on a towel and hope for the best, but I don't think you'd like that. After explaining the differences between resuscitation in the OR and anywhere else, most patients agree to temporarily suspend their DNR/DNI and let us care for them as we see fit. Once the surgery is done and the patient has recovered, their DNR/DNI goes back to normal. Most surgeons won't even perform a non-emergency surgery if a patient completely refuses to be resuscitated, because then they'd have to stand back and watch them die on their table if some potentially reversible problem happened.

I think if everyone spent one day following a doctor around in a hospital, they would all elect to be DNR. Every family has good intentions when they want to keep sweet little granny alive. "Do everything you can," they say. Those good intentions are often the result of guilt and lack of knowledge, because if they saw what it takes to keep someone alive against the body's fervent desire to die, they would strongly consider the DNR. The technology and medicine we have these days are mind-blowing in their ability to keep the body functioning—drugs to squeeze your arteries and drive up the blood pressure, heart/lung bypass machines to take the place of your organs, dialysis machines to clean your blood, ventilators to breathe for you. We can keep little twenty-four-week-old preemies alive; we can stop a heart and use machines to help bypass someone's coronary artery blockages. But these are all scenarios in which a problem is solved. Time is bought until a certain defined outcome can occur. In the case of ninety-five-year-old meemaw who has already coded twice and is on every machine and drip imaginable, there is no end goal. Nor is there one for the unfortunate young people who are brain-dead, whether from trauma or drug overdose. In these scenarios, modern medicine is used simply to sustain a pulse—a bridge to nowhere. The news and media work against us in this regard and usually highlight the very rare successful outcomes after critical illness.

"Our son was in a coma for eight years," the typical story states, "and every doctor told us he was brain-dead and that there was no chance he would recover, but we persisted, and with the help of [insert the deity du jour here] these doctors were all proved wrong." I am truly happy when I see these stories, but news outlets don't show the ninety-nine other stories of similar patients dying a long, slow, agonizing death. I have made it known to my family that if anything were to happen to me and the outcome did not look at all promising, I would not want to be kept artificially alive. I see it all the time and it truly is no way to live.

Surgeons, unfortunately, do a poor job explaining the true risks of a procedure to patients, at least in my experience. They usually hit all the relevant bullet points, from common side effects to rare complications, though some surgeons don't even do this much. Very rarely, however, do they make it clear what these complications would mean to a patient. It is easy to say something like, "The anatomy of your hip fracture makes it relatively straightforward to fix," but harder to say, "You are so sick that if we put a breathing tube in you, it may never come out, and your blood thinners preclude the use of a spinal or epidural," and still harder to make it relevant for the patient—"If we do this surgery, you may not live to see your grandson be married next month." Eliciting a patient's wishes eventually falls to the anesthesiologist, the last hole in the block of Swiss cheese. A patient may elect to undergo a high-risk procedure if it means there is a chance of reducing the severe pain they're currently in, or may defer it if they have a very meaningful event or milestone to look forward to, like the birth of a child or a marriage. This is just another example of how medicine cannot fully be turned into an algorithm, because at the end of the algorithm is still a unique individual with their own goals, beliefs, and dreams.

9. CRACKER BARREL, OR THE BISCUIT BELT

Driving through Yokels-ville during a solo road trip in the dead of night (a.k.a. 5:00 p.m. because of Daylight fucking Savings), hungry, with nary a light in sight, a looming skyscraper of a sign shone through like a beacon of hope: "Cracker Barrel Old Country Store." I had arriven.

Arrove.

...Arrived?

Upon pulling into the parking lot, I thought I accidentally turned into the lot of a nightclub—it was jam-packed with cars, and I'm surprised there were neither police directing the flow of traffic nor bouncers at the doors checking my waist size to see if I was eligible to dine.

The interior was interesting—the first part was a store that sold all kinds of trinkets, tchotchkes, baubles, knick-knacks, paddywhacks, give a dog a *bone. Past all the majestic splendor was the restaurant proper, which was decorated to give a Southern, homestyle vibe. From the brutally decapitated deer mounted above the furiously burning fireplace, to the walls adorned with vintage washboards and chamber pots probably used by the slaves of the CEO's ancestors, everything made me feel at ease—like I was home. Paula Deen's home.*

The menu was gargantuan. And there were three of them: Breakfast (served all day), Lunch n' Dinner (every "and" on the menu was replaced with an "apostrophe N," making it so much easier to read), and a "Light" menu. To quench my thirst, I ordered an Arnold Palmer (a combo of lemonade and SWEET TEA Y'ALL), but with free refills. I was worried I'd start to slur my words and become belligerent. I started scouting the premises for a fine Southern belle to take home that evening and make into a wife. I looked at the woman at the adjacent table, who was working on a glass stein filled with whipped cream. That wouldn't do, so I kept scanning and laid my eyes upon a table full of fine overweight MILFs, sporting short, blond mom cuts, with names like Deb, Mel, and Pam. I rejected these too. I'm just too picky.

I couldn't find Sketti n' Butter listed, so I eventually settled on a country-fried steak—my first one ever! It tasted like a deep-fried dense hamburger, and the gravy on top lacked any range; if I wanted salty cream, I could have asked any of my friends.

For side dishes (Vegetables n' Things), I had the mac and cheese, which was surprisingly good; hash browns three ways, which was not as exciting as I envisioned a three-way to be; and dumplins, which is not only what I dropped in the bathroom after the meal, but also dough in gravy. There was also a plate of cornbread and biscuits and, as the menu so proudly proclaims, REAL BUTTER! The cornbread was mind-blowing—crispy outside, delicate inside, with copious amounts of oil seeping out. Like biting into a delicious abscess on Paula Deen's rectum.

For some reason there was a strange puzzle contraption on the table, which looked like a very small Chinese checker board, with holes you put pegs that look like golf tees into. The puzzle's tagline was, "15 Holes. 14 Pegs. Over 40 years of frustration." Sounds like a summary of my future marriages.

To close out my meal, I just had to get some of that Southern dessert. I got an order of wild Maine blueberry pancakes with blueberry surrup and was not disappointed—the edges of the pancakes were crisp, and the innards were soft like a goose down comforter.

I continued my road trip, satiated and feeling like I was starting to finally fit in down South.

Although I had grown up in New York, I had started feeling the need to get out toward the end of my residency. Everything cost an arm and a leg, driving was an exercise in restraint (from committing murder and/or suicide), and the weather was garbage. There was one snowstorm, nowhere close to the biggest we'd had, that happened to catch the city off guard, causing every bridge and tunnel to get shut down, with people abandoning cars on the roads. I got off work around 2:00 p.m., and my normally half an hour commute started turning into a four-hour one, until I gave up and turned around to spend the night at my friend's apartment near our hospital.

So after basically throwing a dart at a map, I moved down South and was immediately hit with culture shock. The patient population in the South is a world apart from the one I was used to back in New York. Seeing patients over three hundred pounds is now the rule rather than the exception; the largest patient I took care of had a BMI of 90, close to six hundred pounds. There's a reason this area is called the Biscuit Belt. Weights this high have a profound impact on anesthetic and overall medical care, making even the most routine things, such as IV placement and bed position, very difficult. The fatter the population gets, the harder it is for the medical system to take care of it.

After moving here, I realized that my fellow New Yorkers and I had been living like savages, without having accepted the Good Lord Jesus Christ as our savior all these years. Christianity is a big part of life down here. The baseline question is not, "What's your faith?" but "Which church do you go to?" This is relevant during my anesthetic care, mostly because of how amusing it can be.

"It's all in God's hands now," many patients say to me during my preoperative evaluation.

"If it were in God's hands," I yearn to reply, "you'd be long dead, judging by the huge list of medical problems you have. I think God may be trying to tell you something and you're not listening."

A number of these patients frequently ask me if I believe in God, a question I always dread, perhaps more than, "So, how long have you been doing this?" I'm honest and say no, and usually get some reply about how it doesn't matter because God is in me. And He didn't even buy me dinner first.

During my evaluation of a patient about to undergo a cardioversion, a procedure in which an electric shock is delivered to the heart to convert a bad rhythm into a good one, she unsurprisingly called upon a higher power.

"Let's all pray that this is successful and my rhythm gets back to normal," she said. I asked her, surprised, how she knew that prayer was propofol's mechanism of action.

After three electric shocks, we were unsuccessful in converting her to a normal rhythm, and I wondered if it was due to my lack of faith and prayer. The patient had been a good sport, so when she woke up, I checked in on her.

"The good news," I started, "is that we did convert you. You are now Jewish; mazel tov! The bad news is that you're still in A-fib."

She looked displeased, though whether due to her ineffective treatment or her new faith, I will never know.

10. PAPPASITO'S CANTINA, OR A PIECE OF THE PIE

*T*exas. *Land of megachurches, trucks, cowboys, freedom, and xenophobia. Where whatever animal you want turned into boots will be shot on the spot and made for you. And of course, the steak. While in Houston for an anesthesia conference, I did some solo dining at Pappasito's Cantina (not to be confused with Despacito Cantina, Luis Fonsi's first foray into the restaurant world), a Tex-Mex restaurant part of the Pappas group of eateries in Texas. Fun fact: these restaurants were opened by Greek-American brothers, and by adding "-sito" to their name, they magically transformed themselves into Mexican restaurateurs. Greek brothers opening a restaurant by taking the good parts of Mexican culture like guacamole and margaritas, and violently opposing the bad parts, like the bad hombres who make said guacamole and* *margaritas—well goddammit if that wasn't the most American goddamn thing I'd heard.*

I took my seat outside, under the warm radiance of a heat lamp powered by good ol' American petroleum. I was immediately given a large menu, but I soon realized it was just the drinks menu. As I do not imbibe alcohol, that devil's tonic, I settled on a non-alcoholic pineapple cinnamon Agua Fresca, which tasted like an apple pie that fell into a vat of the syrup leftover from a can of pineapple chunks, with more sugar added. I ended up doing some intense Breaking Bad chemistry to dilute it to an amount that wouldn't give me osmotic diuresis. Additionally, a complimentary bowl of tortilla chips and salsa was brought out—it was roast-y and spicy, but over-salted. It was watery rather than chunky, so if you prefer your salsa pouring out the other end of the chip as you pick it up to bite it (what I call the Mexican Salsa Luge), this salsa is for you.

As for real food, I started out with a Pappasito's ceviche, which included avocado, shrimp, scallops, and "fresh fish." It's not like Americans know the difference between anything other than shrimp and salmon, so this honest vagueness on the menu was refreshing. The seafood of the ceviche tasted fresh and pleasant; however, the marinade seemed as if it were pure bottled orange juice, with little complexity of flavors.

I looked through the menu but did not see any clever puns, which these types of restaurants usually have. Where were the Sweet Baby Back Jesus Ribs? The Margaritas on ICE? The Make American Cheese Grated Again Nachos? Truly disappointing.

Pappasito's is known for their Fajitas Famosas, so I settled on the filet mignon fajitas. The steak was cooked a perfect medium rare... at first. The problem with serving meat on a sizzling platter is that the meat continues cooking, so as you eat, you get the whole spectrum from medium rare to rubber. Inherent flaw in the fajita concept. Where is Elon Musk with a solution? The flavors were there though—the thick Maillard-blackened goodies on the bottom were so good I wanted to take a BBQ scraper to it and lick it clean. The sizzling onions and peppers on the platter added great textural and flavor contrasts. Chopped white onions, guacamole, and pico de gallo accompanied the meat and were all fresh and flavorful. A side of beans and rice were thrown in for good measure just in case we weren't sure if we were going to have massive diarrhea later; the beans were rich and stewed with bacon and peppers.

After I devoured my bacchanalian feast, it was naturally time for dessert. The menu was simple: tres leches or churros. However, my waiter José said there was a secret dessert not even on the menu...

"It's like a chocolate cake, with ice cream," he said. " It's pretty good."

You're really selling me on it, José.

I opted for the churros, after which I was asked if I wanted ice cream with them. I told him, "NO WAY, JOSÉ," since I was bordering on exploding already.

Holy shit, why did no one warn me the churro order came with a metric ton of them? I thought these would be some bougie-ass churros, where there would be one and a half of them for the eight dollar cost. But I forgot I was in God's country, the great state of Texas. There seemed to be dozens of churros all intertwined and covered in chocolate, like limbs and bodies in my Great British Baking Show-themed biannual orgies. Churros are supposed to have a perfectly crispy outside and a moist puffy inside; these churros had a poor contrast between exterior and interior. In fact they were almost soggy from the chocolate sauce. The flavor itself was merely passable. I only ate one. In a very un-American gesture, I gave the rest of the plate to a nearby table of eight... who still couldn't finish it.

Now feeling like a goose gavaged for foie gras, I paid my check and walked across the street to the ice cream truck to get some real dessert.

Shit.

It was Texas, and they didn't even have Choco Tacos.

There is a trend across most medical specialties of the rising popularity and prominence of non-physician practitioners. NPs (nurse practitioners), PAs (physician associates, née assistants), CRNAs (certified registered nurse anesthetists). You may even have seen one, instead of the doctor themselves, as your provider when you went to a doctor's office recently. It is unfortunately a touchy topic, because if I say the wrong thing, I could wake up with a horse's head in my bed sheets and a hole in my window with a note taped to a rock on my floor that says, "We're better than you!"

The initial goal of these roles was to expand medical access; ever had to wait six months to see a dermatologist? Well, if we had medical professionals under the supervision of physicians, we could drastically improve that.

In theory.

Eventually, the forces of the free market economy, with strong assistance from the government and base human desires, led to everyone wanting the benefits of being a physician (autonomy, salary) without all that *looooong* medical training. Everyone wants a piece of the pie, and unfortunately, we can't make the pie bigger. The organizations and political action committees representing NPs, PAs, and CRNAs throw propaganda at the public, and more importantly, lawmakers. They say that compared to physicians, they provide equal, if not superior, care, and that they can do it for a fraction of the price. These organizations lobby for independent practice, and often get it in many states, because they know how to play the political game. Physicians are amazing at medical care, but are unfortunately less adept at being politically active. In a way, anything we may do will be met with scorn; if we stay silent, physicians become frustrated and burnt out, while patients receive potentially suboptimal care, and if we become vocal at the national level, we are seen as greedy doctors who just want to protect their own interests and pockets.

Lately, names have been an important point in the march toward non-physician provider autonomy. For example, the national organization representing PAs has changed the name from *physician assistants* to *physician associates*, a change that I suppose in their view will project equality and professionalism. Also, there are now programs, many of which are online, that confer onto nurses or PAs degrees, such as Doctor of Nurse Practitioner and Doctor of Medical Science.[9] These are not medical degrees such as MD/DO, but people with these degrees can *technically* call themselves "doctor." However, I wouldn't have introduced myself as Dr. Antonov to Dr. Stephen Hawking at a theoretical physics conference, since I know my doctorate does not fit into that context. Similarly, having nurses and PAs introduce

---

9 In contrast, there are currently no accredited US medical schools that offer the ability to become a practicing physician completely online.

themselves in a healthcare setting to patients as Dr. So-and-So feels improper at best, and intentionally misleading at worst. Imagine boarding a plane and having someone in a uniform tell you, "Hi, I'm Frank, and I'll be helping fly the plane today," only to find out that this person is not in fact a commercial airline pilot with at least 1,500 hours of flight time, but some sort of pilot assistant who earned their certificate online, with only a few hundred hours of experience (which were all simulation). Apples and oranges, sure, but every field thinks it is immune to encroachment by less-qualified individuals, until it happens. As long as there is money to be had, it is the unfortunate natural drive of people to seek it out while doing the minimum amount of work.

I respect everyone in the medical field, and I especially appreciate the work CRNAs do in my daily practice. In the majority of anesthesia care models, anesthesiologists can supervise up to eight separate rooms (though usually the number is capped at four), with CRNAs providing the minute-to-minute anesthetic care for each patient. The anesthesiologist performs a preoperative evaluation, consents the patient, and comes up with the anesthetic plan, often in collaboration with the CRNA, while the CRNA takes over with the intraoperative management. Anesthesiologists are there and available for all the important parts, like intubation and extubation, and spinal and epidural placement. In some states, CRNAs can practice independently, with no anesthesiologists around, and these are often the scenarios behind the news articles of tragic deaths under anesthesia.[10]

The physician and CRNA relationship is unique, symbiotic, and delicate. CRNAs do most of the procedures, such as intubation and line placement, perhaps even epidurals and spinals, and make sure the anesthetic goes smoothly while the anesthesiologist is seeing other patients and putting out little fires as they come up. They are medical professionals, and not just grunt workers to boss around; teamwork is necessary for the best patient care. Working in this model can be challenging, however, since during residency, anesthesiologists-in-training don't get practice supervising anyone. They are the lowest on the totem pole—everyone's bitch—for four years, and then overnight, when they become attending physicians, they are in charge of supervising multiple CRNAs, some of whom have been practicing longer than they have been alive. Disagreements can arise about the best way to conduct an anesthetic, which I think are a result of the different educational backgrounds; nursing focus is mostly on the intraoperative portion, while the physician focus is on *all* phases of care,

---

10 Some examples: An Arizona CRNA was sued for the death of two separate patients undergoing dental procedures within a year; a Colorado CRNA was charged with manslaughter (the plastic surgeon for the case was also charged with criminally negligent homicide) for the death of a healthy 18 year old woman undergoing an elective breast augmentation.

from preop to after the patient goes home. I want to do everything I reasonably can to make sure you don't have horrible nausea afterward, don't wake up in the recovery room in pain, don't have any kidney damage down the line from suboptimal blood pressure and fluid management, don't have postoperative cognitive dysfunction, and so much more, depending on the situation. Your survival, as I mentioned before, is basically a given.

Eventually, a small part of me died when I realized that I had to weigh requesting a CRNA perform my desired anesthetic, which they may not have experience with, against letting the CRNA perform the anesthetic the way they know well, with potential compromises on certain aspects. Ultimately, if patient safety is not affected, these differences likely matter little in the long run, but can be the difference between a patient saying they had a great anesthetic and saying, for example, that they were vomiting nonstop for a day afterward.

Whole books can be written about the topic of non-physician practitioners.[11] Writers smarter than I can unpack the intricacies involved in the current state of medicine in America. All I will suggest is to be mindful of who takes care of you for some of the most sensitive and important parts of your life. Whether it's

11 Whole books *have* been written about it, such as *Patients at Risk: The Rise of the Nurse Practitioner and Physician Assistant in Healthcare,* by Niran Al-Agba, MD, and Rebekah Bernard, MD.

a PA, NP, CRNA, LPN, DNP, DMSc, or whatever other letter combinations have been created since this was published, know who your provider is. If you are like the majority of patients who are content with their care, that's wonderful, and I'm glad you're at least in the medical system. But never be afraid to ask for the physician, an MD or DO, if you have concerns or questions about your care. We would not have gone through four years of college, four years of rigorous medical school, three-to-seven years of residency, and possibly multi-year fellowships if we didn't care with all our hearts about patient care. We are always there. Though if the political and economic climate keeps moving the way it is, we may not be for long.

11. THE MELTING POT, OR MASKED MAN-DATES

Covid was taking a toll on everyone, me included. I was definitely missing a little romance in my life. So I decided to work up the courage to ask my old friend Pierce (who also came back to NYC after medical school) out on a masked man-date. But where would we find an establishment romantic enough and open to dine-in during the pandemic? My friends, The Melting Pot at a mall out in the burbs was the place. Dressed in my Sunday best (cargo shorts, sandals, and wrinkled tee of unknown origin), I was picked up by Pierce in his Nissan Sentra. I felt as if I were in a limousine—one in which many cigarettes, as well as acid, had been dropped. Like Cinderella on her way to the ball, I was excited.

We arrived at The Melting Pot, a fondue restaurant. Everyone there was living up to the name and was as diverse as they came—there were tan white people, sunburned white people, rosy white people. Upon entering, we noticed the very lounge-y atmosphere, a vast departure from the other American casual chain restaurants I'd been in, and I was impressed until I smelled the combination of cheeses wafting through the air. It smelled as if every woman in the city mistook this restaurant for a yeast infection treatment clinic. Determined to see this night through, however, we made our way to our table. It was a table for five, and we sat as far away from each other as possible, so as not to spew our germs on each other's faces while eating.

The table had two electric burners on it, used for melting the fondues and keeping them bubbly. I'm glad they didn't trust us with gas burners because that place would have long been a pile of ash. When we got our menus, we were confused. There were cheese fondues, salads, entrees, and chocolate fondues. Wait, I thought the fondues were the entrees? And was this price per person or per pot? Was there an abacus I could get to figure out what I wanted to order?

There were many combinations of things, such as 4-course or 3-course meals, as well as a "Back to School" special, which made complete sense to me. Back in the days of my youth, my mother would always freak out the day before school started when she received the list of required supplies. (This is what happened in public school, guys.) From binders, *to crayons, to textbooks, to those goddamn textbook covers that were impossible to put on, to expensive TI-XXS 85 SILVER EDITION graphing calculators. But especially that damn required fondue, which Staples always seemed to have run out of. If only my mom knew about this place back then.*

Eventually, we settled on Fiesta and Cheddar fondues. Obviously, when I thought of fiestas, I thought of jalapeños and salsa, and luckily, that's exactly what was in that fondue, along with cheddar and beer. The Cheddar fondue contained the eponymous cheese, as well as Swiss cheese, garlic, and beer. To my surprise, these fondues were made tableside, a most pleasant spectacle. Served with bread, veggie, apple, and salami dippers, the fondues were deliciously oily and rich, with good contrasts of flavors and textures. The Fiesta fondue also came with tortilla chip dippers, because Mexico. If I had to complain, I would bemoan the softness of the breads; while they were tasty, I felt like a toasted crunch would have been a great textural addition to the meal. In retrospect, I realize the restaurant was covering its bases in case the sugar-eating, non-fluoridated-water-drinking clientele cracked their dentures.

To quench his thirst and vicious alcoholism, my date, Pierce, ordered a "Midnight Lemonade." Our waitress was also the bartender, so he worked his mojo and got her to make it extra strong, making me feel jealous and inadequate.

"It tastes like Wegman's Fruit Punch," Pierce said, "but much better, with alcohol, and with a hint of blackberry."

So basically nothing at all like it.

Next came our entrees. I ordered the Pacific Rim combination because I thought it would come with giant robots and monsters, or at least a rim job, but it only came with teriyaki-marinated sirloin, honey orange duck breast, citrus-infused pork tenderloin, and chicken potstickers.

Everything came out raw, and you had to cook it yourself in the boiling pot of broth on the table. They even provided a "search and rescue" slotted spoon to fetch any lost tidbits. The broth came in a weird pot with a handling device that looked like either a medieval torture rig or a sex toy, or both. The waitress told us it was called "The Romulator."

So sex toy, then.

It was really strange how our waitress took great care and detail to describe to us how long to cook the meats, how not to cross-contaminate, and to call her for extra utensils or plates in case we did cross-contaminate. Why was she wasting our time? In Korean restaurants in Flushing, you just got raw pork that had been sitting an unknown amount of time at the raw bar thrown at you, and you were left to fend for yourself, E. coli be damned. But I sat through her lecture just to be a doll and to try to make Pierce jealous.

The entrees were tasty and were served with a panoply of different sauces. The pork was the weakest of the bunch, but everything else compensated. We were even provided with a special house blend of spices, which I deduced was the exotic combination of garlic powder and salt.

Lastly, the chocolate fondue. I ordered the Cookies & Cream Marshmallow Dream, not to be confused with Young Tight Teens' Chocolate Dream, which is what I had ordered on Pay-Per-View the previous night. It consisted of cookies, cream, milk chocolate, marshmallows, but sadly no dreams. Accompanying it were a great variety of dippers— strawberries, unripe bananas, brownies, marshmallows, pound cake, and cheesecake.

It was the longest meal at that point in my adventures in American casual dining, clocking in at just under two and a half hours, but it gave me time to enjoy life, and to look deep into my date's eyes while he spoke, those dreamy (glazed over), blue (blood-shot) eyes. Looking into them, I could almost see the majestic fjords of Norway, the salmon-filled freshwater streams of Alaska, and the wanton disregard for the federal drug law of Compton. His munchies were satisfied, and as I stepped outside, donning my hazmat suit that I had left over from my "Dustin Hoffman from Outbreak" costume from three

Halloweens prior, I thought about what a beautiful life I have.

The clusterfuck that was the Great Coronavirus Pandemic of 2020 (and could very well still be ongoing when you read this) took a big toll on physicians, and the entire medical system in general. It truly was like the beginnings of all those outbreak movies, where the medical community slowly starts realizing something is wrong, and in no time the hospitals are filled with dying patients while the world goes to hell. No one had the answers, with information and knowledge changing by the hour. People were terrified, and in their hour of need, the medical community was put on a pedestal and recognized for their bravery and service. Every night at 7:00 p.m., New York City residents would open their windows and clap and cheer in appreciation of physicians, nurses, and everyone else working on the frontlines. It was a nice morale boost for us, but it was very short-lived.

The tide turned against physicians in no time. The public's distrust of doctors reached new heights, with people claiming we were withholding certain "magic bullet" medicines, receiving bonuses for each patient that died from Covid, overplaying the severity of the disease, and on and on. A patient walked through my hospital's front doors during the height of the pandemic as I was there picking up a food delivery for my overnight shift (thank you, food service industry workers) and asked the security officer for a mask. He replied that he could not give masks away, since, of course, there were critical shortages at the time.

"Man, the hospitals and doctors ain't even trying to help us," she said in disbelief.

Racism and xenophobia suddenly became in vogue again, thanks to the origins of the virus and the political climate at the time. My (Thai) wife was walking back to our apartment from her car after a long shift of treating Covid patients, when a mom and her young daughter were walking by. The mother pulled her daughter close and hurried away, telling her, "Stay away from that Chinese lady." Little did she know this "Chinese" lady was the one that would be managing the ventilator if she contracted Covid.

Celebrities and internet denizens magically became virologists and physicians overnight via Facebook University, and often spread misinformation about the pandemic, even disparaging Dr. Anthony Fauci—the man who literally wrote the book on medicine that every med student uses.[12]

In addition to the public battle, we also struggled at work. I went from playing musical chairs on the *Titanic* to being an orchestra player on the doomed boat, trying to support everyone as everything around me sank. Supply shortages abounded in the beginning of the pandemic, with our medical governing bodies

12 Dr Fauci is the second author of the textbook *Harrison's Principles of Internal Medicine*, which is on its 21st edition as of 2022.

telling us just to use a bandana over our faces if we didn't have an N95 respirator. These N95s, which were meant to be worn once per patient and discarded, were now being reused for days before being "reprocessed." Ventilators and morgues were in short supply as well, with teams working on how to ventilate multiple patients with one ventilator, and multiple mobile cold storage trucks parked outside hospitals to house dead bodies. Simply seeing a patient was burdensome, as it required putting on booties, a hat, a gown, a mask, eye protection, and gloves and then taking it all off when finished, before doing it all over for the next patient. We faced death often, with patients dying alone in their rooms since no visitors were allowed, for everyone's protection.

One small benefit that came from the whole mess was that sick-leave policies at work were re-evaluated. Obviously, no one wanted an employee, including a physician, to come to work if they had coronavirus. I myself took the leisurely CDC-recommended ten days off when I contracted it the first time in March 2020. This was so jarring because physicians are expected to operate at 100 percent every day. Even back in medical school before I had any real responsibilities, I felt the pressure. I had to take my end-of-semester exams while battling a raging gastrointestinal illness; I would ask for a break in the middle of a test to go shit my brains out (while a chaperone stood outside the door making sure I wasn't trying to cheat by faking diarrhea noises with a Super Soaker), return to finish the test, then go home to lie down in a cold sweat for an hour before returning to the lecture hall to finish the remaining exams.

Sick leave and time off are rare; patients often guilt physicians when they take vacations, half-jokingly claiming we're abandoning them, and physicians themselves feel that if they don't work, the entire medical system will just collapse. While this issue of physician mental and physical wellness has not been resolved yet—at one job, I asked what I should do if I contracted coronavirus, and my colleague said that I had better be on a ventilator if I didn't come to work—it is at least being talked about more.

I'm not sure if physicians will recover any shred of respect from the public; we are conveniently there when needed but get shit on the other times. At least I got some brief benefits from the pandemic: there was no traffic (a rarity in NYC), and I got to skip to the front of the Costco line. Now if you'll excuse me, I have to jump into my pool filled with toilet paper and Covid death money.

12. TEXAS ROADHOUSE, OR DRIVE A GEO METRO

N*othing screams "colon full of meat" like my alma mater New York University, but I suppose Texas Roadhouse is a close second. I went to this particular restaurant chain at the behest of a friend, who claimed that it was a better version of Outback Steakhouse. With such astronomically high praises, you better believe I had similarly high expectations. It didn't matter that I was with great new friends and enjoying our pre-Thanksgiving time —if the food wasn't plentiful and cheap, everything would be ruined.*

I love meat in and around my mouth, and you bet your gluteus maximus this place hit the spot. Even having dined in the popular NYC steakhouse classics like Peter Luger's, Ruth's Chris, and Club A, I was still impressed by Texas Roadhouse. Right at the entrance, amidst traditional American decor like coloring books, random license plates, neon beer signs, and stereotypical images of Native Americans, was a giant barrel of peanuts. My accompanying friend took one, cracked it open, ate the nut, and dropped the shell like a spent casing on the floor. I was aghast—why would he litter in such a fine establishment? Not to worry, he told me, assuaging my fears, you're supposed to do this. I felt like a whole new path of life opened up to me. I immediately began eating peanuts and dropping the shells, leaving a trail behind me like Hansel and fucking Gretel.

Now having a return route to use if I got lost in the labyrinthine restaurant, I felt confident enough to proceed forward. As my companions and I were seated, I noticed a mini-trough of peanuts on the table and continued to machine-gun fire out my cartridges of nuts; I noticed an empty mini-trough later, but goddammit, this is 'Murica, and I'll drop my peanut shells wherever I damn well please. We were quickly provided fresh-baked bread, the rolls sweating oil almost as much as the diners around us. They were soft, fatty, and slightly sweet, and the rolls were pretty good too. The accompanying cinnamon butter complemented them well. Having engaged in the equivalent of injecting pure cow lard into my veins, I was ready to engage in that seductive dance called "ordering food."

The waitress asked what we wanted to drink.

"I'll have your freshest tap water, please," I said, trying to be cute. She was immune to both my charms and my boyish good looks, for she just gave me a quizzical "I-don't-know-what-you-just-said-but-I-hate-you-already" stare.

"So... just tap water, right?" This waitress was very perceptive.

I noticed something similar to Outback's famous Bloomin' Onion on the menu, called a Cactus Blossom. I appreciated that the corporate kitchens decided to name their food very appropriately, as this onion was quite petite—a flower not yet in full bloom, but just beginning to blossom. I was also glad they took great care of this flower, watering it with a copious amount of oil to keep it healthy.

Lucky me—the entrees lived up to the standards set by the appetizer. My Sirloin Kabob, a valiantly-attempted pastiche of Middle Eastern elements, was a collection of sirloin cubes (some chewy, some soft, because who doesn't like some variety in their lives?) with some onions and peppers served over gummy rice.

The sides really stole the show, however. I thought maybe I wanted to be a little healthy that evening, so I ordered the green beans, but Texas Roadhouse whipped out its meaty member and slapped me across my face with it, as the beans had been stewed with bacon and tasted like Miss Piggy's sports bra.

Similarly, my friends wanted some light dressings on their salads, but, nope. This time Mr. Roadhouse and his friend Paul Newman whipped out their respective penii (that's right, Newman's Own!) and double-teamed us by squirting out onto our salads the best fatty bottled dressing on the market.

Having finished my meal, I followed my trail of shells out (not before adding a few more shells on the table for my lovely waitress to dispose of), mounted my faithful steed, and rode off into the sunset, wondering to which casual dining spot the winds would take me next.

Most people are as comfortable talking about money as they are about their secret desire to try butt stuff, which is to say, not at all. As a result, there are many misconceptions about physician salaries. I think the prevailing assumption is that we get paid a boatload of money and buy loads of boats with that money, but that is mostly wrong. To understand the physician financial situation, we have to start back at college.

After completing an undergraduate degree, many future physicians are already loaded with student loans. The average American college graduate leaves with their degree and about $30,000 of student loan debt, but that does not account for the fact that many medical school applicants come from higher-tier schools, which are often private, rather than public state schools, and thus have much higher tuition. I graduated from a private college in NYC, which cost over $40,000 per year in tuition alone at the time, and just like every other American college, it gets more expensive every year. I didn't need to pole dance my way through college—I had the fortuitous double whammy of being both smart and poor, which resulted in me receiving a nice scholarship and graduating with only a few thousand dollars of debt.

The average medical school debt is much higher, however, at over $200,000, not including pre-medical or college education debt. My own bill was a little higher, and that was at a state medical school, which was significantly cheaper than a private one. Med students often have to take out larger loans in order to cover their living expenses, since there is little time to have any meaningful job. Additionally, all the exams and certifications we have to take to become and stay practicing physicians are exorbitantly expensive. Throughout med school and residency, I paid almost $10,000 in exam fees alone. Every year, I pay thousands more dollars to maintain board certification and a bunch of required licenses.

During residency, physicians finally start making a salary. Around $60,000 per year on average.

"Hey, that's not bad!" you're probably thinking.

But when you factor in sixty-to-eighty (stressful)-hour workweeks, it comes out to about $15-20 dollars an hour. Close to New York City minimum wage. Most residents do not have the means to start paying off their loans during this time, opting instead for numerous income-based payment programs. These minimum payments aren't even enough to make a dent in the interest that accrues every month, so at the end of residency, my debt had ballooned. Compound interest giveth, and it taketh away.

By the time my wife and I became attending physicians, we had a combined debt of over half a million dollars. We were thirty years old and finally started making real money. Meanwhile, non-medical friends, who started working after college (or even earlier, if they didn't attend college), had almost ten years of savings and real life under their belts. They had houses whose mortgages they could comfortably afford, they were starting families, they were taking vacations. All of these real-world things, the processes that ground you to society, are delayed for physicians. This lost time is perhaps the biggest cost of all and one that is not appreciated by most people. Doctors suddenly find themselves in their thirties, emerging bleary-eyed from the dark prison of medical education, with no real-world education or experience. Remember how well that worked out for the crow-loving librarian Brooks in The Shawshank Redemption? Spoiler alert, he couldn't handle being out of jail after being incarcerated for so long and killed himself.

Salaries vary from specialty to specialty, and even within them as well, depending on a multitude of factors, so take specific numbers with a grain of salt. On average, procedural and glamor specialties, such as plastic surgery, dermatology, ophthalmology, and orthopedics, pay higher than the perhaps more important but less glamorous specialties such as pediatrics and family medicine. The salaries for anesthesiologists usually run from $300,000 to $500,000, though I am currently making less than that, while salaries for pediatricians can be $150,000 to $200,000. Productive and skilled surgeons in private practice can rake in millions of dollars a year, though if you've ever appreciated a pair of beautifully enhanced breasts, I'm sure you'd deem the salary justified.

These are definitely big numbers. Physicians are without a doubt top earners in America, though often not the "1 percent," especially the lower-paying specialties I mentioned. It is hard for physicians to complain about money when they make two to ten times the amount the average American household does in a year. And yet, we have reasons to be upset. The combined monthly student loan minimum payment between my wife and me is $6,000 (and that's if we want to stretch it out over ten years with the resulting tens of thousands of dollars of interest accruing), which is a significant chunk of our paycheck. I have to take this into account in addition to all the other expenses associated with someone in the prime of their career, even though I have started only relatively recently. Mortgage for a house in a good school district for my kids. Childcare. Catch-up on almost ten lost years of retirement contributions. Healthcare expenses associated with growing older. Life insurance, so if I die, my family can continue to live comfortably. Disability insurance, so if I injure my hand in an unfortunate masturbation accident, I can still make some money. Umbrella insurance, so if some asshole finds out I'm a doctor and wants to sue me for a well-timed "accidental" slip on my sidewalk, I won't lose everything. And of course, Netflix and Amazon Prime.

The "Keeping up with the Joneses" force is strong for new attending physicians. The desire to finally start living a life that has been delayed for so long. Physicians often run into problems with this, buying expensive cars and houses and living luxuriously, running on more borrowed money. The other end of the spectrum is continuing to live like a pauper until all of your loans are paid off, which has its own appeal. If you skip that Starbucks, drive a Geo Metro, and don't make any memories with your family, you'll pay off your loans in no time. The prospect of being free of debt is exhilarating, but the extremes that are advocated to achieve it make the whole thing comical. I can be struck down at any moment, either by cancer, a car accident, a plane crash, or whatever, and I know I won't be looking back on my life saying, "I'm sure glad I ate only Cup Noodles and didn't go on any vacations with my family so I could pay off my loans a little earlier." There is a middle ground, and it's the job of every physician to find it for themselves. I'm still working on it.

13. MEDICAL TV BULLSHIT

Medicine on television is often inaccurate. As a medical professional, it bugs me to see my field misrepresented. I'm sure lawyers scream at their screens during dramatic courtroom scenes, and I'm sure every other profession has things they nitpick when they see their trade being shown on the silver screen. Here are some of my gripes.

Despite what many of the popular medical shows depict, there are no hot orgies happening in the call rooms, or furtive hookups occurring in closets. At least not routinely. And at least not with me. If this *does* indeed happen, why the hell didn't I go to a residency program like that? It would have definitely made the four years fly by. Everyone knows of someone who has done the deed in a call room, whether with a nurse, a co-resident, or themselves, but that's more the exception than the rule. At least I hope so, for my pride's sake.

You ever notice how doctors in medical shows seem to do the job of about three dozen people? *House* was especially egregious in this regard. The medicine doctors would see their patient, realize something was amiss and order an MRI, and *operate the machine themselves,* interpret the imaging and decide a biopsy of some organ was indicated, and *perform it themselves,* then go to the lab and actually *look at the slide under a microscope,* have a revelation that maybe something in the patient's environment was causing the issue, and just *leave the hospital* and break into the patient's home, basically turning into *CSI* for a bit. In reality, doctors barely have time to even do their minimum required work because of all the pressures put on them. Also, do you think doctors know anything about any specialty other than their own? Everything in medicine is so specialized at this point, due to the ever-increasing complexity of technology and knowledge, that everyone stays in their own little worlds. Does the patient have a heart? You better consult cardiology. And as for the *NCIS*-style scenes of doctors doing detective work, I can imagine that there are some laws that would get broken doing that. And to be honest, as much as I would love to analyze semen stains in a patient's house, I have better things to do.

As an anesthesiologist, I am always annoyed at how medications are depicted on TV. The classic shot of a man suddenly clutching his chest in pain, scrambling for his magic pills, spilling all of them before finally popping one in his mouth, and letting out an instantaneous "ahhhh" before it has barely had time to hit his tongue, is mostly bullshit. Any medicine needs time to work, especially when it is in pill form—it takes time to get down to your stomach, shed whatever coating is on it, dissolve, get absorbed into the bloodstream, and finally reach the target receptors. The only instance that may be close to the above example is someone having anginal chest pain and taking sublingual nitroglycerine to relieve it; the medicine has to be dissolved under the tongue for rapid absorption, but every TV person just swallows it down. Additionally, the relief happens on the order of a few minutes, not a few fractions of a second.

The "Gas Man" in *Dumb and Dumber,* while eating in a diner with Harry and Lloyd, accidentally swallows rat poison meant for them, and within a few minutes, convulses and dies. Check, please! While certainly hilarious, the scene loses some credibility when you know what rat poison is. Usually, rat poison is a blood thinner—very similar to the warfarin your grandpappy takes for his atrial fibrillation—and takes quite long to work. It exerts its effect by interfering with vitamin K's role in the clotting pathway of blood, which is not a fast process, and kills the rats by bleeding them out from within. So, what would have happened in reality in this scene is an uneventful lunch, with the Gas Man noticing some blood on his toothbrush and in his stool the following day, then dying from either brisk gastrointestinal bleeding or a massive hemorrhagic stroke. Not as funny.

Numerous movies and shows use poisoning as a comedic device. In *Only Murders in the Building*, Steve Martin's character gets furtively slipped an unknown drug that incapacitates him, leaving him only able to hilariously flop around and slur an occasional word. Similarly, Leo's character in *The Wolf of Wall Street* overdoses on drugs and is unable to speak, and can only do flops and wriggles as he memorably tries to open his convertible's scissor doors
using his feet. Where are these magic drugs in the real world? While these nameless movie drugs offer great opportunities for physical comedy, there is no drug that can selectively paralyze certain parts of your body while still allowing you to think clearly and breathe. There are indeed paralytic drugs we use in anesthesia, but these paralyze everything, including your

diaphragm. If you took these drugs by themselves, you would have a nice few minutes of total body paralysis, aware of your impending death from lack of oxygen and unable to do anything about it. In the above *Wolf of Wall Street* example, the drugs in question are actually Quaaludes, but those are similar in effect to Xanax or alcohol and lead to sedation, sleep, and cessation of breathing in an overdose, not Leo doing a Scotty 2 Hotty-esque worm across the sidewalk.

Injections are problematic in film as well. In *Pulp Fiction*, John Travolta's character infamously slams a syringe of epinephrine directly through the sternum and into the heart of Uma Thurman's character, reviving her from her heroin overdose. Multiple ridiculous problems there: the force needed to penetrate through the breast bone is huge, so much so that little guns and drills exist to get special IV lines into bones, and Uma would have been better served by a slow and controlled puncture between ribs instead; stabbing the heart blindly with a force large enough to penetrate bone would likely cause trauma and lead to bleeding into the pericardium (the super-thin layer surrounding the heart) or the chest cavity; instead of epinephrine, which would not do much to undo a heroin overdose, the drug naloxone should have been used to reverse opioids and get Uma breathing again.

Trauma and resuscitation are generally poorly depicted on TV, often exaggerated for dramatic effect. I'm sure you've seen many scenes of some poor schlub being rushed into a trauma bay with paramedics pumping his chest on the stretcher, everyone running around yelling things like, "STAT!" and doctors instantly figuring out what's wrong after a cursory exam, and then maybe extracting a bullet and dropping it with a loud, satisfying, *clink* into a metal basin. While some things are usually accurate—trauma is a time-sensitive situation with a patient sometimes arriving on death's door with people attempting resuscitation—I mostly cringe at the added drama. The shearing off of the patient's clothes is accurate, not to ogle their willy as you may think, but to evaluate for any hidden injuries. The removal of a foreign body miraculously solving all problems, however, is so stupid that it's hard to imagine who believes that. When someone gets shot in their abdomen, the bullet can blow through intestines, spilling out shit into your abdomen and causing massive sepsis; or it can damage the aorta and other blood vessels, leading to rapid exsanguination; or puncture various organs like the kidneys and liver; or sever the spinal cord leading to paralysis, or any combination of the above. Removing the small bullet fragment would not solve any of these issues, and, in fact, tons of people (veterans in particular) walk around with retained bullets and metal fragments in their body, since the act of attempting removal likely would have caused more damage than simply leaving them be.

In a well-run trauma situation or code, the room should be calm and serious, rather than loud and chaotic with supplies flying all over the place. (Though in reality, codes sometimes do become messy affairs, especially with improperly trained practitioners leading them.)[13] The chest compressions shown on TV are always of poor quality—they should ideally be at least two inches deep to really compress the heart, and allow for full recoil to allow the heart to fill back up with blood—likely due to the fact that performing real chest compressions on an actor would be extremely uncomfortable and dangerous, to put it mildly.

I have a big issue with the outcomes of codes that are depicted on film. Mostly, it seems that the results shown are favorable; little Joey gets successfully brought back to life after a car hit him on his bicycle after only a few rounds of compressions, and everyone lives happily ever after. This leads to a

---

13 A *code* is medical lingo for a situation warranting immediate chest compressions, defibrillation, airway intervention, or all of the above, such as when a patient's heart stops or goes into an improper rhythm, or when they stop breathing. A patient can be described as having *coded*, or doctors rushing to them to *run a code*.

public perception that CPR saves lives with a high success rate. The real outcomes are much grimmer, however. Survival rates after CPR in hospitals are well below 50 percent, and out-of-hospital CPR is even less successful, with rates not much higher than 10 percent. This also doesn't account for the quality of life after survival—oftentimes these patients are brain damaged from the lack of oxygen during their cardiac arrest, or have severe organ damage for the same reason. This disparity between popular misconceptions of CPR success and the reality of it has led to a trend of permitting family members to watch the resuscitation occur on their loved ones. When you are ushered from a room and don't see what is happening to grandma, your imagination runs wild and you hope for everything to be done to save her. When you are watching it happen, hearing the ribs crack and break under the force of the compressions, seeing the anesthesiologist forcefully shoving a breathing tube down her throat, hoping for a sign of life even after twenty minutes of the same cycles, you are more likely to understand that there is little chance of meaningful recovery from it.

The public's overconfidence in medical intervention leads to sensationalist news stories that subtly insult medical professionals. As I mentioned earlier, every so often, an article pops up detailing how some sick patient, someone's *daughter*, for God's sake, finally woke up from a long coma after her courageous family didn't listen to all the naysaying doctors and pushed for every intervention to be done. These stories obviously make doctors look like villains, but they never mention how in the vast majority of cases, those types of patients don't make it. Physicians would love for every patient to recover fully, but we also take into account suffering and futility, and it weighs on us greatly when we feel we are performing futile care that is only prolonging the patient's eventual demise. The exception is made to look like the rule.

Anesthesiology itself is not often the subject of films or TV, and is rarely shown or mentioned at all. I mean, I'd be pretty bored as a viewer watching the anesthesiologist do sudoku puzzles and figure out the bed controls for an hour. What *is* shown is usually laughable. Patients' eyes are often shown unprotected, which is a setup for a corneal abrasion and severe eye discomfort after the surgery. Their bodies are often completely exposed with no forced air warmers on, which would lead to hypothermia and a host of poor outcomes. In many scenes, the anesthesiologists seem to perform a mask induction, which involves inducing anesthesia via gas through the breathing mask, but this is usually only reserved for small children who cannot tolerate the placement of an IV, which is the more standard route of inducing anesthesia. After induction, the anesthesiologist is sometimes not even in the OR —that probably would lead to too crowded of a shot, but, hey, it's just cruise control at that point anyway, right? If they *are* in the room, there is often no sterile drape between them and the surgeon. Many times, the breathing tube is either unsecured, which could easily lead to inadvertent extubation, or not a breathing tube at all, but some other tubular medical-looking thing the production designers had on hand. (A particularly egregious example in something I've seen is a suction catheter in place of a breathing tube, which would leave you unable to deliver any oxygen at all, but at least you could suck all of the air out of the lungs if you wanted to kill the patient quickly!)

One of my favorite movies with a tangentially anesthesia-related scene is 2004's *The Punisher* with Thomas Jane. I don't know why this film stuck with me all these years, since it was universally panned, but I'm thinking a big part of it is how handsome Thomas Jane is. A lesser reason is one scene in particular, in which the Punisher is about to torture some poor schlub to get some desired information out of him.

The Punisher stands out of sight behind his victim, who is naked and strung upside down, and describes to him the torture method he will use. A blowtorch, so scalding hot that it instantly sears the nerves, making it so the victim doesn't feel any pain at first. And then, just the feeling of cold, as his body slips away into shock and unconsciousness. As the Punisher interrogates the victim in his prerequisite gruff Marvel hero voice, he clicks his metal blowtorch igniter, producing the characteristic *fwoomp* of a fire starting. When he doesn't get the answers he wants, he pretends to hold the blowtorch to the victim's back by first searing a piece of steak nearby to get a sizzle and the smell of burning meat, and then slathering his skin with an ice-cold popsicle. The victim yells out in surprise and perceived pain, begging him to stop as he gives up his secrets. The Punisher returns to the front of the victim and thanks him as he shoves the popsicle in his mouth.

I thought this was so comical and smart when I saw this scene as a teenager, even before knowing what I know as an anesthesiologist. The scientific basis of this scene is the spinal cord nerve pathways. There are numerous nerve tracts that carry different types of sensory information, including pressure, proprioception (the feeling of knowing where in space your body is), touch, pain, and temperature. Those last two—pain and temperature—actually travel together in the spinothalamic tract.

This comes into play on a daily basis for many anesthesiologists during Cesarean deliveries. Usually, we perform a spinal anesthetic, where we place a thin needle into the patient's back to access the sac (he-he) the spinal cord is wrapped in and inject the space with a local anesthetic. This makes the patient numb for the duration of the surgery, allowing her to be awake for the birth of her baby. But while she won't feel sensations of sharp or cutting pain, she will still feel pressure, pulling, and tugging, since those sensory fibers travel on a completely different pathway from the ones that transmit sharp pain.

How do we know if the spinal anesthetic is working before the surgeon cuts into an awake patient? Do we stab her belly with a scalpel, yelling, "CAN YOU FEEL THIS?" That's a tad barbaric. In reality, many anesthesiologists channel their inner Punisher, using the knowledge Thomas Jane taught them about the intertwined nature of pain and temperature transmission to test their anesthetic. We can use an ice cube or a cold alcohol swab and swipe it over a part of the patient that is not anesthetized, such as the arm or the forehead, and ask her if she feels cold. That's her baseline. Then, we swipe our cold object over different parts of the belly, asking if those sensations feel different than the ones on the forehead or arm. If the patient denies feeling cold, then we can safely assume she won't feel sharp pain there either, since the two fiber types travel together. The best and most reliable answer from a patient is her asking if we started yet, indicating no feeling at all, and while I dread that answer in the bedroom, I appreciate it in the OR.

"Isn't science fun?" Thomas Jane's character asks his victim after he deepthroats him with a SpongeBob popsicle.

Indeed it is.

14. I LOVE IT AND I HATE IT

My friends, I have no more funny nor meaningful shit left to say. I'm still in the beginning of my career, though remember: the start of a doctor's real career is likely ten to fifteen years later than yours. Medicine has taken and continues to take a toll on me, and I'm starting to feel my age for the first time; did you know you can use the number of grunts uttered while bending over to tie your shoes in the same way you can count rings on a tree to tell how old something is?

I hope I've shown you that anesthesiologists don't just sit around in the OR all day playing Candy Crush and moving the bed up and down, though some amount of both does happen when appropriate. Moreover, I hope you see that physicians are not infallible gods, but people—sometimes vulgar and offensive people, with their own unique sets of interests and goals.

I often think about whether I would do the whole medicine thing over again. I do enjoy anesthesiology and don't think I'd pick any other specialty, though I'm sure I would have made a fine enough physician in any field. But I wonder whether I would have even started the whole medical journey in the first place? That's a tough one, because I just don't know what else I would do. In what other field do you have the privilege of holding in your hands someone's life while getting reasonably reimbursed for it? It is a special profession, and it is a huge part of my identity. I love it and I hate it, all in the same day. If you catch me outside looking lovingly in your direction, I promise it's because I'm probably admiring your veins and wondering how big of an IV I can put in them.

As for the fruit of my loins, my future generations, I would warn them about the realities of medicine if they had a desire to pursue it, since I myself did not comprehend them when I was starting out. I would leave the rest in their hands.

Then, I would take them to a nice, casual chain restaurant.

ACKNOWLEDGEMENTS

This book is the result of decades of experiences that led to me becoming a doctor. This life has been filled with countless friends, co-students, co-residents, and colleagues who have helped my personal and professional development in one way or another. I thank all of these people for being there for me and for educating me. I especially thank the select few who read this book in advance and offered their feedback. Even the ones who said, "Oh God, why would you ever want to publish this?" You know who you are.

Thanks to the people who helped with the technical aspects of this book: my editor Stacey Kopp for improving the grammar and flow of the story, my illustrator Daniel Weiner for his great artwork, and my cover designer for putting everything together to make an eye-catching book cover.

I am constantly thankful to the patients I take care of every day. Even though some make me tear my hair out (just stop fucking smoking, for the love of

God), they are the reason physicians do what they do, and believe me, I know how cliche that sounds.

I thank my wife for being by my side throughout this life of medicine. My wife puts up with a lot of my shit, but as you have just read, I had a lot more of said shit that needed a creative outlet. Her journey through medicine deserves its own book, for she has gone through more trials and tribulations than I have. Kids during residency? A minority female in medicine? Dealing with me? Give this woman a medal. I give my deepest love, admiration, respect, and gratitude to her.

My kids are such a bright spot in my life, and I hope when they're older they'll read this and ask me questions about it, such as, "How exactly did Mom fit into your journey?" and, "What is autoerotic asphyxiation?" Thank you, my boys, for helping me see I'm not completely selfish.

Lastly, I thank you, my reader. It is risky and frightening to put one's creative work out there in the world, so regardless of whether you liked it, hated it, or thought it was okay, thank you for giving it a chance. A creative life is a good one, friends, and I encourage everyone to chase your own creativity. Just don't cancel me after reading this book, please.

ABOUT THE AUTHOR

Zach Antonov, MD is an anesthesiologist and amateur stand-up comedian who loves to write, share jokes, and knock people out. As the author of *I Watch You Sleep*, Zach hopes to entertain readers with a humorous and witty collection of real-life tales of sending patients to sleep and (hopefully) waking them back up again. Zach grew up in New York City, took a detour to upstate NY for medical school, and returned to his hometown to complete his anesthesiology residency. He now practices medicine in the southern US. In his free time, Zach enjoys writing for medical journals and blogs, as well as all things cooking and food-related.